Eugene J. McCarthy

Complexities and Contraries

Essays of Mild Discontent

Harcourt Brace Jovanovich, Publishers
New York and London

"For the Want of Horses," © 1977 by The New York Times Company, originally appeared in *The New York Times* as "A Return to Horseplay" and is reprinted by permission. The following are reprinted from *The Washington Star*, with permission, copyright reserved: "The Cockerel Step," May 8, 1977; "Message of the Irish Character," Mar. 19, 1978; "The Old-Time Meaning: What Was Good for Tom and Alben," Aug. 14, 1977; "The Most-Wanted Best Man," Jan. 1, 1978 as "Why the Best? Isn't Good Good Enough"; "Jimmy Carter's Cookie Cutter," July 24, 1977; "A Reasonable Translation," Jan. 22, 1978; "Hogs or Cattle," Dec. 18, 1977 as "A Choice of Methods"; "God's in His World," Oct. 21, 1977; "Old Counselors May Fade, but Not Away," Feb. 12, 1978; "Debt-Ceiling Time in the Valley," Oct. 23, 1977; "Is Justice Deaf? Not Blind?," Feb. 5, 1978 as "Now a Spiffier High Court"; "More and More Things We All Could Be Protected From," Dec. 11, 1977; "The Sacking of Sir Peter Ramsbotham," May 29, 1977; "Say It Ain't So, George!," July 17, 1977; "The Columnist's Power of Rash Judgment," Jan. 8, 1978; "Some Thoughts on Having Given Scandal," Jan. 15, 1978; "A Strange Inquiry," Sept. 11, 1977; "A Festival of Hope," Dec. 25, 1977

Library of Congress Cataloging in Publication Data
McCarthy, Eugene J., 1916–
Complexities and contraries.
1. United States—Politics and government—1945-
—Addresses, essays, lectures. I. Title.
E839.5.M28   973.92   81-48016
ISBN 0-15-121202-3   AACR2

Printed in the United States of America

First edition

B C D E

In memory of Senator Philip Hart

He was in ways a man out of his proper time, a man meant
for the Age of Faith, or at least for the declining years
of that age, when men like Thomas More could make their
last defense, beyond the civil law, in religious belief.

Contents

Contents

Contents

Preface

This book is a selected collection of essays, articles, and columns written over the period of approximately four years beginning soon after the inauguration of President Carter and ending soon after he left office in January of 1981. It is not a running commentary on the Carter administration and not all the topics are political. Most of the writing was inspired, provoked, suggested (not elicited) by contemporary events; by actions, words of politicians, editors, television commentators, and real persons. All, I thought, had significance when first written, in immediate application, but also continuing longer-range worth and applicability when considered in a framework of history, experience, and ideas.

All were meant to be taken seriously. I did not seek in my writing to achieve a particular style or mood, but hoped for a happy accommodation between subject matter and writing. As a defense against critics and reviewers who may come searching my motives and divining my mood, let me declare that where choice or distinction could be made, I intended to be ironic rather than satirical; skeptical, not cynical; and optimistic rather than pessimistic, according to the distinction of Chesterton, who wrote that a pessimist was one who saw how bad the state of the world was and despaired of doing anything about it, whereas the optimist saw how bad things were but did not give up hope of change and of improvement.

It may seem that inclusions are too heavily weighted with references to animals and with images dependent on animal behavior. The use of such metaphors has a long and well-founded tradition in American politics. A major contributor to that tradition was Abraham Lincoln, who, in the famous Lincoln-Douglas debates, never referred to Douglas as a Senator, but as a "toothless lion," "a frightened bear," and a "cuttlefish." After Gettysburg, he did not say to his General "You let the enemy escape," but "Meade, it seems to me you shooed the geese over the river."

Alexander Pope, who in his much-quoted couplet ". . . presume not God to scan./The proper study of mankind is man" obviously meant to be modest and humble, is in fact somewhat arrogant, or, if not, somewhat irrelevant. A wiser man has said, "The proper study of mankind, and especially of politicians, is animals."

There is a special good in a book of this kind. Once essays and articles such as these are printed in book form, the author must assume that they are generally read, and known, and may then turn to other themes and topics for future speeches, articles, and books.

The man bent over his guitar,
A shearsman of sorts. The day was green.

They said, "You have a blue guitar,
You do not play things as they are."

The man replied, "Things as they are
Are changed upon the blue guitar."

—Wallace Stevens,
"The Man with the Blue Guitar"

The Cockerel Step

The cockerel step by which the light
Shortened the sleep of earth and night.
—VERNON WATKINS

To understand the Carter Presidency, it is necessary, or at least helpful, to know what a "cockerel step" is.

It is the step that marks the young, insecure rooster, as distinguished from the established cock of the walk, or of the yard. The cockerel step is marked by three stages, separable and definable. In the first stage, the rooster raises one foot, holding the leg close to his body, suggesting great restraint and growing tension. During this stage, the rooster looks thoughtful—and confident. In the second stage, the tension is released (détented, in the new language of diplomacy). The foot is thrust forward very positively and aggressively, and then brought to a stop, well above the ground. In the third stage, the leg is retracted, the claws relaxed. The foot is drawn back slowly and put on the ground—at just about the same spot at which the first stage of the step began. If the first step was taken with the right leg, the second, similar in all respects, will be with the left.

Thus, in the campaign, and after, Mr. Carter denounced the Internal Revenue Code as a disgrace to the human race. He had lifted his foot from the ground. Then he

3

suggested radical, if not violent, changes. The tax rates would be changed, loopholes closed, capital gains treated as ordinary income. Interest paid on home mortgages no longer would be allowed as a deduction. Overseas income would be taxed differently. The valleys of the code would be raised, and the mountains and hills would be lowered. The income tax code would be made straight as the way of the Lord.

Ah, but hold a moment. The leg with the threatening claw has been extended, but not yet put down to claim new territory. It hangs there, suspended like the blade of the guillotine. Slowly, the leg is retracted. The threatening claw is drawn back. How about settling for an increase in the investment credit, and a tax rebate of $50 per person, or per some persons? But hold again. Not so fast or so far. Let us reconsider the rebate and also the investment credit. Down comes the foot, in the same old scratch mark.

And now the other foot is lifted. This time, the subject matter is control of inflation. Inflation is the cruelest tax. It comes like the wolf in the night; it attacks the old and the defenseless. It is silent, too, and secretive, like the moth and rust. It must and shall be stopped. The foot has been raised. And now the forward thrust: Threaten wage and price controls, free trade, and antitrust action. Break up the oil companies. Reform the tax code so as to get at the special interests. But hold again: The leg with its frightening claws is drawn back. Break up the oil companies? But how? Vertically? Serious problems. Horizontally? More serious problems. How about doing it on the diagonal? Or perhaps aim at reduced hospital costs, and a balanced budget in 1980, and regular monthly meetings "between the Chairman of the Federal Reserve, myself,

4

and my chief economic advisers in an effort to achieve better coordination of monetary and fiscal policies." And now the foot is gently lowered to the ground, a little behind the spot from which it was first raised.

But the other foot is already rising. Government reorganization and bureaucratic reform, economy and efficiency in administration—all of these and more are the targets of the next step. Everyone waits. And now comes the forward thrust. The number of agencies, bureaus, commissions, and other definable units of administration in the federal government will be reduced from whatever the present number is. (No one is quite sure—probably between sixteen hundred and seventeen hundred, depending on definitions and criteria.) No matter: The number will be reduced, ready or not, to two hundred. There will be no overlapping, no feather-bedding, no waste. A veritable drum roll before the execution. The leg is extended to full length, the claw clenches and unclenches. Bureaucrats cringe behind their desks; clerks barricade themselves behind the filing cabinets. The walls of the Department of Agriculture show slight cracks. Even in the Pentagon, a slight tremor is felt. The ratio of officers to men is to be changed. And in the navy, more captains at sea, fewer in the office of the land-based Chief of Naval Operations.

But hold again, not so fast. The White House staff must be increased "to answer the volume of mail." The President has gone "directly to the people." They are responding. He must respond. He has circumvented the Congress, or vaulted over it. The President has demonstrated his credibility by having his telephone calls screened or filtered by "the most trusted man in America," Walter Cronkite. Don't write or call your member of Congress.

Go directly to the White House. Obviously, this new relationship between President and people, if it is to be developed properly, requires an increase in the White House staff. Perhaps congressional staffs should be cut. And we do need a new, top-level energy coordinator, James Schlesinger, and a staff to go with the coordinator. The foot has been drawn back. Decently and with dignity, it has been put down again just about where it came from.

There are similar steps in waiting—on energy, disarmament, the problems of the cities, and so forth. The essence of the cockerel step: action, but not movement.

Message of the Irish Character

It is difficult for those who are not Irish to understand the Irish character. It appears to them to be full of contradiction. They confuse complexities with contraries.

The Irish wake is not an accident. There is a strong undercurrent of sadness in any Irish joyous celebration and, on the other hand, even in Irish mourning, there is an element of joy.

This seeming division characterizes the history of the Irish people, as it characterizes the Irish personality. The Irish character has not been formed and proved in one short test or in one shining hour. It has been slow-tested and proved in a long and bitter history. In defeat and oppression and suffering.

The Irish character, as a result of this testing and trial, has been marked by a great longing and aspiration for freedom. That longing and that aspiration have been expressed in the five great loves of the Irish people.

First is their great love for country—for the soil of Ireland, for its towns and its people. So great is this love and longing that the greatest punishment set for Columkille, the saint, was that he could no longer set foot on Irish soil.

So we have, all of us, in a sense remained exiles whenever we have been away from Ireland. Like Columkille, we can say, "There is a grey eye which ever turns to Erin. What joy to fly upon the white crested sea, and to sight the waves breaking upon the Irish Shore. To return to Ireland where the song of the birds is so sweet and the clerks sing as well, where the young are so gentle and the old are so wise, where great men are noble and the women so fair."

The second great love of the Irish is their love for religion—for the things of the spirit, for the faith. At the time of the coming of Christianity, the Irish spirit was willing and ready. Saint Patrick came and was received without martyrdom. The same cannot be said of the other lands: not of Rome, not of Gaul, not of the East, not even of the new continents found across the sea.

The third great love is the love of learning, whereby the Irish kept alive the flame of knowledge and the pursuit of truth in those centuries when in all parts of the world, learning was despised and trod upon. Ireland has not produced the greatest scholars in the history of the world. She has produced scholars who have done what needed to be done.

The fourth great love is that of political freedom—a love that sustained the Irish in standing against the Danes and the Normans, the Tudor armies, the hosts of Cromwell, and all the soldiers of the king. The ancient Gaelic law recognized this in forbidding the seizure by justice, in any house of any Gael whatsoever, of his books, his sword, or his harp. For books were the symbol of his intellectual and spiritual freedom. The sword was the symbol of his political freedom, and the harp was the symbol of all things to which the human heart aspires. These are American aspirations, too.

The fifth great love is that of poetry and song—a love so strong and deep and so consequential that as late as the fifteenth and sixteenth centuries, English rulers imposed special penalties on bards, minstrels, rhymers, and genealogists who sustained "the Irish lords and gentlemen in their love of rebellion and other crimes"; and the soldiers of Cromwell broke the harps found on the walls of Irish cottages at the time of the invasion.

The Irish view of the good society was best described by the ancient Celtic monk Cadoc the Wise, who wrote in the sixth century the "Song of Hate." It was not really a song of hate, but rather a song of grief, in which Cadoc catalogued all of those bad things, all of those undesirable things, that he wished to see removed from the life of man. The "Song of Hate" runs thus:

> I hate the judge who loves money,
>   and the scribe who loves war,
>   and chiefs who do not guard
>   their subjects, and nations with-
>   out vigor.
> I hate houses without dwellers,
>   lands untilled, fields that bear
>   no harvest.
> Landless clans, the agents of
>   error, the oppressors of truth.
> I hate him who respects not father
>   or mother, those who make
>   strife among friends.
> A country in anarchy, lost learn-
>   ing, and uncertain boundaries.
> I hate journeys without safety,
>   families without virtue, law-
>   suits without reason.

Complexities and Contraries

Ambushes and treasons, faults in
    counsel and justice unhonored.
I hate a man without a trade, a
    laborer without choice, a society
    without freedom, a society with-
    out teachers, a false witness
    before a judge, the un-
    deserving exalted to high position.
Fables in place of teaching,
    knowledge without inspiration.
Sermons without eloquence, and a
    man without a conscience.

The Old-Time Meaning: What Was Good for Tom and Alben

Concern over the Vice-Presidency began early in the history of the nation. Even the first Vice-President, John Adams, was unhappy in the office. He described it as "the most insignificant office that ever the invention of man contrived or his imagination conceived." Adams wrote, at a time when the selection of the Vice-President by the electoral college was a most serious matter, since under the original constitutional system, he was the second choice for the Presidency and likely to succeed to that office.

Almost immediately following the Washington-Adams administration, the Vice-Presidency became a pawn in partisan or factional manipulation. In 1803, the Twelfth Amendment, which joined the vote for President and Vice-President, was approved by the Congress. Two years earlier, a proposal to abolish the Vice-Presidency had failed by a vote of 19 to 12 in the United States Senate.

The effect of the Twelfth Amendment was to lower significantly the status of the Vice-President. No longer would gifted men seeking the highest office become Vice-President, or "President-in-Waiting." The balanced ticket of special partisan value took over. In the years following, Vice-Presidents were not looked on as Presidential material. After the Twelfth Amendment was adopted, only two Vice-Presidents ascended to the Presidency by popular election. (Several others reached the Presidency because of the death of a President, then won election in their own right.)

At the beginning of this century, the sad state of the office was reflected in Mr. Dooley's expression of wonder as to why "ivrybody runs away fr'm a nommynation f'r vice prisidint as if it was an indictment be th' gran' jury?"

Not even Franklin Roosevelt, who gave new meaning to the Presidency, offered to give new meaning to the Vice-Presidency. When he ran for a third term, he dropped his running mate of two successful previous elections, John Nance Garner, and ran with Henry Wallace. Following the third term, during which Wallace—on his own—attempted to give new meaning to the office, Roosevelt dropped him for Harry Truman, who was content with the old meaning. Alben Barkley, by all reports, was happy in the Vice-Presidency under the old conception.

Concern over the happiness of the Vice-President became a national concern, and "giving new meaning" to the office a matter of commitment by the Presidential candidate in the 1952 Eisenhower campaign. It was said that in the new administration, Vice-President Richard Nixon would be given special assignments and responsibilities never before borne by a Vice-President. The extent of this grant of power and responsibility was brought into question during a 1960 Eisenhower news conference. When asked for an example of a major Nixon contribution to his administration, President Eisenhower replied, "If you give me a week, I might think of one. I don't remember."

President Kennedy gave special administrative assignments to his Vice-President, Lyndon Johnson, and consulted with him. Yet, Lyndon Johnson was not a happy Vice-President. And President Kennedy reportedly said that the Vice-President was consulted on everything that worked out well, but that he was slighted or left out of those consultations that were less than successful.

Vice-President Hubert Humphrey acknowledged that he was an active agent of President Johnson, and appeared to be satisfied. But, in his recent book, he expressed dissatisfaction over the manner in which he was treated by President Johnson.

Vice-President Agnew, who was described as Nixon's Nixon, which should have been a fulfilling experience, now murmurs in the gates about the role which he played in that administration. Gerald Ford held the office too briefly to give it any new meaning. Nelson Rockefeller left no mark on the office.

Now we have the Carter administration, claiming that it is giving the Vice-President new responsibilities and is giving the office a new, new meaning. To date, the newness has been evident in two ways. The first is in Vice-Presidential travels. Vice-Presidents of recent administrations have traveled. But, as a rule, they have not been sent off until after the new administration has been well settled in office and they have become restless. Vice-President Mondale traveled earlier than other recent Vice-Presidents.

The second manifestation of new meaning was the Vice-President's submission, following a Presidential request, of an election reform program. The Vice-President acted quickly. It was almost as though he said to the President, "I'm glad you asked me to do that." Within a few weeks after receiving the Presidential request, the Vice-President submitted his proposal. He made three major recommendations. The first: easy, if not instant or universal, voter registration, called by some the Richard Daley Memorial Voter Registration Act. The second: federal financing of House and Senate elections, following the pattern of public funding of Presidential elections. The third: abolition of the representative electoral college process, substituting for it direct election of the President and Vice-President by popular vote.

The first two proposals have not been accepted by Congress. The third, which is likely to be rejected, has not been taken up by either the House or the Senate.

If proposals like these are the likely product of giving Vice-Presidents new responsibilities, the practice should be discontinued. And if the office cannot be abolished, as was attempted in 1801, the old meaning and constitutional role of the Vice-Presidency should be restored. That role is limited to presiding over the Senate and voting in the case of a tie.

Thomas Jefferson properly understood the role of the Vice-Presidency. He found it a pleasant office, giving him the time, he said, in the winter to contemplate philosophy, and in the summer to study nature. During his years as Vice-President, Jefferson invented a hemp beater. He won a French prize for his design of a better plow. He devised a leather buggy top, and reportedly invented the dollar, the dime, and the penny, as well as the $10 gold piece and the silver dollar.

That was a constructive Vice-Presidency. It prompts the following refrain about the office: "What was good for Tom and Alben/Is good enough for me."

The Most-Wanted Best Man

The search is on for the most-wanted man. The search is not being conducted by the FBI, but for the FBI—to find its new director. The procedure reportedly followed by the administration is to have the Attorney General recommend ten possible appointees. From among the ten, the President, after due consideration and reflection, will make his choice.

This method is an application of recent FBI practices. Many years ago, the bureau used to name someone as the most-wanted man—and possibly someone else as the second-most-wanted man. Whether the first was wanted more or wanted first, and the other less or later, was never clear from the language. More recently, for reasons not given, the most wanted are thrown into a group, usually designated as the ten most wanted. The conclusion is that these ten are wanted, either collectively or individually, more than any other persons. Catching any one of them is a mark of special credit, for each one must be most wanted.

We can safely anticipate that the President's choice of a new FBI director will be declared superlative—the best of the ten. It will be difficult to make him an absolute best, because we already have been told, and more or less have accepted, that Judge Frank Johnson, who had to turn down an appointment to head the bureau because of ill health, was the best man for the job. So what we will be getting this time is the best of the ten second-best.

In recent administrations, it has become the general practice to appoint none but the best. The old saying that "a good man is hard to find" seems to be outmoded. Beginning with Dwight Eisenhower, Presidents have accepted only the superlative "best," not being content even with appointing better persons than those who had served in previous administrations. If Thomas Marshall (Vice-President in Woodrow Wilson's administration) were in politics today, he would not dare to say that what America needs is a good five-cent cigar. He would be forced to say that what America needs is "the best" five-cent cigar.

In this modern spirit, President Carter wrote of his approach to the Presidency in a book called *Why Not the Best?* Consistent with that theme, the President has labeled nearly every one of his choices "the best"—the best Vice-President, the best director of OMB, Judge Johnson the best head of the FBI, and so forth.

One of President Nixon's favorite words was "greatest." President Johnson spoke modestly of establishing "The Great Society." The move from great to greatest is easy. Members of the Kennedy administration, when referred to as "the best and the brightest," accepted the adjectives with modesty.

In the same spirit, when special committees are set up today, whether by government or by business, they are called blue-ribbon committees. Blue, of course, is the color of the ribbon given to winners of first place in horse shows. It would be a pleasant relief, and would be more honest, to have a President occasionally designate a committee as a red-ribbon committee (second place) or a yellow-ribbon committee (third place) or a green-ribbon committee (fourth place) or a brown-ribbon committee (just for coming).

I do not recall President Truman's ever having appointed a search committee, certainly not a blue-ribbon committee. There was never a great talent search during his administration, with the President waiting anxiously for the select list to be submitted to him, and with the country standing by like the faithful waiting for white smoke from the Vatican announcing that a new pope had been chosen.

President Truman kept his judgments and credits well within the limits of the positive degree. He seldom ventured into the comparative, and never into the superlative. He did make distinctions in his judgment of persons, but the positive was all that he needed. "Good" was the commanding adjective. Some persons he described as simply good—a good man or a good woman. Some he described as "damn good." (That was high praise.) On the other hand, he thought that some persons were "no good" and that others were "no damn good." It was good language, well spoken.

Jimmy Carter's Cookie Cutter

The neutron bomb is not so bad. There are a lot of things to be said for it.

First, it would reduce what has come to be called the collateral damage of nuclear bombs now in our arsenal—that is, the damage to civilian areas resulting from blast and fire.

The neutron bomb would release large quantities of neutrons that would incapacitate and kill many of the enemy within minutes. (But enemy troops on the periphery of the target area would die a slow death of convulsions. No bomb is perfect.)

It would not destroy buildings, automobiles, tanks, or other military equipment. After removal of the dead persons and animals, the buildings and equipment could be occupied and used within a short time.

The monkeys used in one series of neutron tests were prepared by being taught to run on a treadmill. After they were subjected to neutron radiation, they were placed back on the treadmill. Evidently, their wills were not immediately destroyed. Their performance after exposure varied, but all of them died within 132 hours.

According to some advocates, the neutron bomb would be "more credible" than the nuclear weapons presently in our arsenal, described now as "normal nuclear weapons" or "regular nuclear weapons" or "conventional nuclear weapons." (They have not yet become "traditional.") It is argued that Presidents who might hesitate to use one of these more primitive instruments, because of incidental or collateral consequences, would not hesitate to use the more precise and cleaner weapon.

The neutron bomb is also more purely scientific than other instruments of death. The death it causes is "integral." It destroys the cell structure, especially that of the central nervous system, of those who come within its range.

Accepting the more sophisticated and scientific way of death has long been the mark of progress in Western civilization. Thus, in disposing of enemies of the state, the guillotine was preferred over the executioner's axe. The guillotine was more scientific; it used gravity rather than human strength; it was more accurate; its collateral effects were minimal. Later, the electric chair and the gas chamber were adopted as offering "more humane" ways of execution. So why not neutron exposure, at least in conditions of war? With the exception of the banning of poison gas after World War I, and the banning of bacteriological weapons in an international agreement signed in 1972, there has been little hesitation over using the newest scientific knowledge for military purposes. Why hesitate now?

The neutron bomb is not so new in any case. Familiarity breeds, not always contempt, but acceptance. Defense officials say that weapons similar to the neutron bomb have been in the U.S. arsenal for years. For further assurance, they report that when James Schlesinger, then head of the Atomic Energy Commission, took his family to the site of an underground atomic test in 1971, the device tested was an "enhanced radiation" warhead similar to the neutron bomb. So why worry?

Moreover, the bomb has been developed under carefully controlled conditions. Defense officials tell us that it has not been tested on human beings, but that on the basis of tests with animals, estimates of its effects on humans "have been synthesized." The bomb will work.

The new weapon has been gently nicknamed by its designers; it is called the cookie cutter. We should be able to become accustomed to that name. It calls up images of mothers, warm kitchens, the smell of baking, and cookie forms—diamonds, hearts, clubs, spades, gingerbread boys, Dutch girls, rabbits, and (best of all) the small, odd-shaped pieces that escaped the cookie cutter.

Weapons should have names, and nicknames. We have had the Bowie knife, the Patton tank, the Sherman tank. Why not name nuclear weapons after those who introduce them into the "mix" (as it is called) of our arms package? We could have called the atomic bomb the "Harry," and the hydrogen bomb the "Ike." Now we have the "Jimmy Carter cookie cutter."

Despite all of its positive qualities, the neutron bomb won't do. Destruction of buildings, visible evidence of conquest, is necessary to victory. (One of the reasons we lost in Vietnam was that people were all we had to destroy.) Carthage was razed. General Sherman, on his march from Atlanta to the sea, did little more than what would now be called "collateral damage." Moscow was burned at Napoleon's approach, and so on.

Furthermore, the neutron bomb will not do because it does not lend itself to television coverage. A war without crumbling walls, rubble, flames, fleeing women and children will not do.

The Celtic Mystery
of Kings, Presidents,
and Poets

Each year, as Saint Patrick's Day approaches, I resolve that I will not do an Irish column for the day. Each year, something happens that compels me to break that resolution. Either I discover that some special virtue in the Irish character is misunderstood or not even recognized by the non-Celtic world, that an Irish tradition is being ignored, or in some cases, that the Irish character is being falsely attacked.

This Saint Patrick's Day I am forced to take up the matter of President Carter's misuse of poets. There is an Irish tradition going back to the Druids, and continuing through the Christian era, down to modern times, that holds that poets deserve special respect from kings and others who hold political power.

Poets were believed to hold special powers. The master poet of all Ireland in the seventh century, one Shanahan, on finding one day that rats had eaten his dinner, spoke these words: "Rats have sharp snouts/Yet they are poor fighters."

The words alone, according to report, killed ten rats on the spot.

The same Shanahan conducted one of the first hunger

strikes recorded in history against King Giare, who had sent the poet down from his high table.

"I yielded to the outcry of my courtiers," said the King in his defense. "Bishops, Soldiers, and Makers of the Law/ Who long had thought it against their dignity/For a mere man of words to sit amongst them."

The King tried every device to induce or force Shanahan to give up his protest, but to no avail. The honor of the poets was at stake. There were rumors of revolt against the King. Shanahan's followers and fellow poets urged him to persevere in his fast. Finally, the King took off his crown and gave it to Shanahan, who then restored it to the King. Never again in the reign of King Giare was the poet sent down from the high table.

Antagonism between politicians and poets is as old as history. Poets of other cultures have resented their treatment, especially neglect, by politicians, but none have fought back as vigorously and as continuously as have the Irish poets.

Some eight hundred years after Shanahan, poets of Ireland were singled out by an order of Queen Elizabeth of England that "rhymers and genealogists" should be suppressed. George III is reported to have said that "poets and painters" were the greatest enemies of the State. And sixteenth-century English poet Edmund Spenser wrote of the Irish poets of his time that "none dare displease them for feare to runne into reproach through their offense and to be made infamous in the mouthes of men. . . ."

William Butler Yeats, continuing the battle into the twentieth century, wrote these words of his enemies: "But weigh this song with the great and their pride/I made it out of a mouthful of air/And their children's children shall say that they lied."

President Carter may not have known about the power of the Irish poets, but as a student of recent Presidential history, he should have noted what did happen to Presidents who displeased the poets.

John Kennedy was attentive to the poets. He invited Robert Frost to write a poem and to read it during the inauguration ceremonies. In speeches during his campaign and during his years in office, President Kennedy regularly quoted poetry. The poets honored him in their works both before and after his death.

Presidents Johnson and Nixon did not heed the poets or show respect for their works. The poets of America responded in the best tradition of the Irish bards.

One, Robert Bly, who had written in praise of John Kennedy, described President Johnson in a short poem as "shovel without a handle," and wrote another poem entitled "Johnson's Cabinet Watched by Ants."

Richard Nixon, needless to say, was not spared by the poets. Henry Taylor wrote of Nixon in a poem called "Speech."

> I crouch over my radio
> to tune in the President
> thinking how lucky I am
> not to own a television.

And another poet, Jay Meek, describes President Nixon watching himself on television in these words: "He has been watching himself too long;/His eyes click and roll like fruits in the windows of a gambling machine."

President Carter got his administration off to a good start by including poet James Dickey in his inaugural program. But, from that point on, his relationship with the poets has gone downhill, to a low point early this year when some seventy-five poets were invited to the White House.

That meeting must be faulted by poets on at least three counts:

First: The invitation came not from the President but from the First Lady, suggesting that poetry, like tea, is for ladies and for afternoons.

Second: Poetry was included by the White House in the category of "the performing arts." Poets do not consider themselves to be performing artists, nor do they look on poetry as a performing art.

Third: The invitation fell far short of making up for the fact that no poets had been invited to the week-long Camp David meetings of last summer; meetings that included all of the same classes of people, religious leaders, military, and lawmakers, who had urged King Giare to put down Shanahan from the high table, and also other kinds of people, even including television commentators, the ultimate offense to the poets.

It is late for President Carter, but he may still have time to save himself by responding to the poets, as King Giare did to the Protest of Shanahan.

A Reasonable Translation

The translator of President Carter's remarks at the Warsaw airport has been most unfairly treated by a critical press and by State Department officials. It is unlikely that any translator, even with an advance text (especially if the text were written by Zbigniew Brzezinski), and even though he had not been wet and cold, as Steven Seymour says he was, could have done any better than Seymour did.

Any reasonably careful student of what was said and done before the Presidential trip might well have translated Carter's reference to leaving Washington into "I have abandoned my country."

Consider first that here was the President of the United States in Poland. A President who had said that he would not leave the country until Congress passed a satisfactory energy bill. He had never set a limit on how long he would wait. He might well have been initiating a secular version of the Vatican Captivity, a policy of self-imprisonment adopted by the popes from 1870 to 1929 in protest against the Italian government's annexation of Rome.

But Congress had not acted by the time the President

went abroad. The energy crisis, as announced and defined by the President in March of last year, had not been alleviated. Moreover, the country was suffering some of the worst early-winter weather in its history.

Under these conditions, what was a translator to think? A President who had left the country, despite what he had said about not leaving, who had left it without any forgiving message to the Congress or any reassuring message to the people as to why he was traveling (there was even some question about the countries he would visit), might well have been judged to have abandoned his country, at least temporarily.

Having made that judgment, it would follow easily for the translator to believe that the President physically desired Poland. Language experts say that the Polish word used in the translation suggests physical or carnal desire. (The last would be difficult to conceive.) But if the President had indeed abandoned his country, he might have been seeking asylum, or even another country to govern. Why not Poland?—a country that he seems to have discovered as having as much (or nearly as much) freedom as Gerald Ford tried to say it had during the Presidential debates.

Apart from the Polish visit, and the translation, President Carter is often hard to understand even in English.

What does the President mean when he says to the people of the country, as he often does, "I love you"? Is it pure spiritual love? Is it sentimental love? Is it mere lust of the heart? Is it physical or carnal, or is it something else?

Whom does he mean when he says, "We love you"? Mark Twain wrote that no one should use the undefined "we" excepting the king of England, the archbishop of

Canterbury (or possibly the pope), or someone with a tapeworm.

How would one translate into Polish his statement: "What I liked about being in the submarine is that it was embryonic"?

As a rule, not too much should be expected of Presidential interpreters or translators. When they fail, they should be granted amnesty or pardon. They should be treated in the manner which, in George Seferis's poem "Three Mules," Queen Eleanor recommended for the mule Margarita, which had slipped while carrying her. The Queen died of a broken neck in the fall, but returned as a spirit to say, "Don't wrong the mule. I was full of the will of God. A beast can't bear that much weight."

So, too, of the translators of Presidential speeches.

Why Not Celibacy for Presidents?

It was certain to come: the comparison of the wives of Presidential candidates as potential First Ladies (or assuming that a woman may be elected to the Presidency, of potential First Gentlemen). The competition has already been introduced tentatively in the Democratic party's preconvention contest, not by the party but by the press, following the publication of the magazine interview in which Joan Kennedy said she thinks she is better qualified to be First Lady than is Rosalynn Carter.

The daily commercial press, after publicizing the magazine article, did not itself editorialize on the issue of which woman is best qualified to be First Lady. Rather, it turned the matter over to those who write letters to the editors, especially, by count of letters published, to women letters-to-the-editor writers. The results were not unlike those reported to have occurred in those primitive societies in which captured women were turned over to the female members of the tribe.

In the 1960 Presidential debates, only the Presidential candidates were included in the debates. In 1976, the Vice-Presidential candidates were added to the show. We can anticipate that something new will have to be added to enliven the interest in the 1980 campaign. And that following the conventions, and the selection of the Republican Vice-Presidential candidate, the only business remaining to be accomplished in either convention, the question of the qualifications of the spouses of both the Vice-Presidential and Presidential candidates will again be raised.

The League of Women Voters, which has assumed, or been given by some unknown authority, the power to determine who is to participate in Presidential campaign debates and to establish the conditions for such debates, may be moved to add this third debate between wives of the candidates.

It would not be wholly unreasonable to do so, as candidates almost without exception declare in their campaigns that their wives are their special confidantes and advisers. Jimmy Carter, for example, said that Rosalynn was "closest to his consciousness." It might be helpful to the electorate to get a better idea of how persuasive the spouses could be and some idea as to what kind of advice they might give to their husbands.

There is precedent of concern over the character and qualifications of spouses in fields other than politics. Major corporations, for example, make careful evaluations of wives before promoting husbands to high corporate offices. Now that women are rising in the corporate world, the corporations undoubtedly are also evaluating husbands. In an interview published several years ago, one corporate official raised a question as to whether corporations that invest a great deal in bringing young executives along the corporate trail should not exercise greater foresight in advance of marriages by promising corporate employees, counseling them as to what kind of person, as husband or wife, might best serve the long-term interests of the corporation.

A congressional inquiry discovered the fact that the navy (this was before women were admitted to military service) required in advance of promotions of junior officers not only an evaluation of the officer but also of his wife. It was never made clear in the inquiry as to who evaluated the wives—senior naval officers, or their wives.

The State Department, not to be caught short, required ratings of the wives of Foreign Service officers. Under congressional questioning, the personnel officer of the State Department, when asked about the evaluations and the extent to which he relied on them in making appointments, reported that he had not found them very useful, and that after studying many reports, he had concluded that every Foreign Service officer was married to the same woman, who was intelligent, virtuous, socially acceptable, patient, loyal, dedicated, attractive, etc.

An alternative to this increasingly complex approach to picking a President would be to look to religious history, with the rule of celibacy for its clergy. This long-standing rule is being challenged within the Catholic Church. Compromise positions are being offered, such as allowing priests to marry, but to insist on celibacy for bishops and for the pope. One can assume that if ordination of women is approved, similar variations may be applied. In its application to politics, House members might be allowed to marry, but celibacy required of senators, and certainly of the President.

Presidents are beginning to claim powers previously reserved to religious leaders: a kind of infallibility, reflected in statements such as: "If you knew what the President knows and had to carry the burdens of the office as he does," you would agree with him. And moral leadership, as evidenced in President Nixon's statement that the President is the moral leader of the country, and a comparable statement by President Carter that only the President can speak the moral judgment of the country to the rest of the world.

Celibacy would seem to be a small price to pay for the possession of such powers. Certainly, if it were required of Presidents, it would simplify the electoral process.

The Elements of Style:
A Volatile Mix of
Modern-Day Metaphors

William Strunk, Jr., as every right-writing American knows, was the professor who taught E. B. White English 8 at Cornell University in the year 1919. Strunk is also the author of the book *The Elements of Style*, reissued with an introduction and some editing by E. B. White. The book is, according to White, "a forty-three page summation of the case for cleanliness, accuracy, and brevity in the use of English."

Strunk, the critic, were he with us now, should be asked to start at the top, and look first at the writings and speeches of President Carter.

"We must evolve and consummate our foreign policy openly and frankly," President Carter has said.

"How now?" Strunk would surely say. "An evolving foreign policy? Possibly, but it would take a long time. Surely more than one four-year term. Evolution is a slow process. But consummating it openly and frankly, not only bad English but a sure case of indecent exposure. Why not try something like 'open covenants, openly arrived at.' "

And another Carter offering: "We must stop the despoiling or derogating of the land or of the air or the water within which we must live."

Despoiling air and water is difficult, Strunk would surely note. And living within air (possible for birds) or within water (possible for fish) or within land (possible for worms)—but all difficult for people, except for very short periods of time.

But "derogating land, air, or water," Strunk would say, "I do not understand." And he would surely red-pencil President Carter's statement that "we will go forward from this convention . . . ready to embark on great national deeds." Deeds, he might note, are "fragile barks" not to be embarked in on life's tempestuous seas. He would lift an eyebrow at Carter's statement that he would "insist avidly" and "very seriously deplore," noting that deploring is usually a serious act, if not a very serious one.

If Strunk were to leave the Presidential texts, hoping for solace in the writings and statements of other than politicians, looking for comfort among the members of the writing press, and beyond in higher-paid realms of television reporting, he might well be brought near despair.

For he would read that "imponderables" are at work in China. That there is a demand for credit that will not be "assuaged." That the budget is "full of ironies," that "weather problems plagued the Christmas crunch" (Walter Cronkite). That Congress was "mesmerized by an impasse which had become a death trap of legislation," and also that the country was spinning its wheels in a "domestic impasse."

He would hear of the athlete who "deserved a lot of accolade" (possibly to go with Gatorade). And of another who was "knocked oblivious." He would have to

learn a new mathematics to understand a newspaper report of a military unit that was decimated by one-third,
and of another that was totally decimated (which could
mean that a whole ten percent was gone or that ten times
ten or one hundred percent was taken). He would be
told that in one week in one city there were "five arsons"
and a "series of culminations."

And at a higher level of reading, ponder the image of
Washington presented by David Broder as writhing "in
the pain of its paralysis." Writhing paralysis must be a
new and distressing kind of paralysis. He would be called
upon to interpret this sentence by Rod MacLeish that
"Nixon and Johnson, aided by archdukes like Henry
Kissinger, rammed their wills through a befuddled Congress."

Finally, he would be brought to the newest entry in
communications, something called, by television observers, the closer or the stand-upper. It is the concluding
comment of television correspondents, usually a short
sentence. Sometimes, it is only a phrase, or a question,
spoken, after the news story has been presented. It is supposed to give meaning to a story, or take meaning away,
or in some way put the stamp of the reporter's judgment
on the story.

Here are recent examples. CBS correspondent Lesley
Stahl, after reporting on President Carter, added this
closer: "Some say that the President's increasing stridency
is beginning to look like desperation."

Strunk surely would ask first what desperation looks
like, and then question whether stridency, a quality of
voice, could possibly look like something. "Some" is a
favorite source of reflective commentary for Ms. Stahl.
He, she, or they may soon be quoted, as in "Confuscius
say."

Another recognized master or mistress of the closer is Judy Woodruff of NBC. She does not quote "some," but rather goes to the "question being asked." After noting in a recent broadcast that public opinion polls have shown that one of President Carter's "strongest points is his image as a decent man," she added, "The question being asked is whether Mr. Carter himself is undercutting his strongest selling point." Ms. Woodruff does not say who is asking the question; it seems to be floating about. Nor does she explain how one undercuts a selling point. This would puzzle Strunk, as would a closer, by Tom Pettit, in which he, in a story about Senator Kennedy, said, "If Kennedy makes a miracle for Carter, that would not hurt him for 1984. Nor would failure to make a miracle." Making a miracle, Strunk would surely note, is more difficult than performing one, or than simply not making one, and add that "verbs do not go well with miracles."

Hogs or Cattle

Just as there are more ways than one of killing a cat, so there are more ways than one of getting action from Congress. Yet, President Carter seems to believe that there is but one way, which is to be applied to all cases. In this, he follows Lyndon Johnson's example.

President Johnson's methodology was drawn directly from his experience in driving cattle, and it worked quite effectively until its final application to the war in Vietnam.

The basic technique in driving cattle is to start the herd very slowly and quietly, being careful not to alarm the animals or startle them. When stirring a herd to movement, cowboys sing "Get along, little dogies" and the like. Once a herd is started, the speed of its movement can be accelerated until, as the cattle approach the loading pens, the drive becomes a stampede. The stampede allows little space or time for reconsideration of one's course.

Thus, in the early stages of what was to become a deep involvement in Vietnam, President Johnson spoke reassuringly of not having American boys do for Asians what Asian boys should do. He asked Congress to pass the Tonkin Gulf Resolution largely as a vote of confidence and with assurances that it gave no new powers to the President. Eventually, the escalation of the war became a near-stampede; and those who opposed it were criticized, in the language of the cattle drover, for having "cut and run." (Cutting and running is the only way to get out of a stampede.)

President Carter's farm experience apparently does not include the handling of cattle. The Georgia experience is largely restricted to moving hogs.

Now, the method for driving hogs is quite the opposite of the one used for cattle. To start pigs, it is necessary to panic them. Hog-drovers beat on pens and pig troughs; they shout at pigs in Latin, crying, "Sui, sui. . . ." So much for the start, which is the easiest part of the drive. Once pigs are started, the pace of the drive should be slowed down very subtly, so that the pigs arrive at the desired point just as they are about to come to a halt. If pigs are moved carefully in this way, they usually walk right into the pen or loading chute as though they had discovered it.

A great mistake in driving hogs is to start them fast, as prescribed; then allow them to slow down; and then try to accelerate the drive. The attempted speed-up can end only in disaster. The pigs go off in every direction, and even turn and come back through the legs of the drovers. In a large field, it may take days to reassemble the herd, quiet it down, and prepare it for the next panicked start.

Obviously, President Carter knows how to start the hog drive. He has presented every major issue with initial flourish and great outcry: the energy crisis, welfare reform, tax changes and reforms, even the Panama Canal. But after the start has come the slowdown and then, with the attempted speed-up, the scattering of the herd.

Either the cow method or the hog one, or both, have application to Congress. The choice depends largely on what the issue is and which body of Congress the President hopes to move. As a rule, the hog-driving technique (the initial panic, with the subtle slowdown) is better for the Senate. Hogs are noted for being more independent than cows or, for that matter, sheep; and they give evidence that their reputation is deserved. The cattle-driving technique usually is more appropriate as a way of getting action in the House of Representatives.

There is also the antelope response, which occurs only under unusual circumstances and which, once put in motion, cannot be reversed. It is not easily planned or even anticipated. It happens usually when there is a panic for reform, as in the passage of the federal election act. The late Senator Eugene Millikin of Colorado used to say that when the panic is at its height, there is nothing left to do but paint a white splotch on the seat of one's pants and run with the antelope.

There are, of course, some issues and problems that are best presented and considered by the Congress within the range of human response and human methods.

Another Good Season

Another baseball season is about to begin. It will be a good season. Every baseball season is a good one. The strength of the game is proved year after year, despite expansion teams (which in recent years have done no worse than the old St. Louis Browns used to do season after season) and changes in rules and record-keeping. The designated-hitter experiment seems to have done no lasting harm.

The livelier ball has been introduced, but the relative strength of hitters and pitchers seems to be in reasonable balance. The cowhide cover, proposed as a substitute for horsehide, has been rejected. The hardwood bat has survived the onslaught of aluminum and plastic substitutes.

Team loyalty is adequate. Team spirit and loyalty have never been as important in baseball as in other sports, in any case. Baseball teams do not carry chaplains, as do some football teams. They do not gather, kneeling or standing, in a group to pray or hold hands before the game, as basketball teams do, but proceed decently from locker room to dugout to playing field.

Baseball, forever resilient, has adjusted to night games,

to artificial turf, to the Astrodome, and to Charley Finley.

The reason is not a matter of accident. It is a matter of essence, for baseball is different from other games. Its strength is inherent, metaphysical. Why? First, the game has a singular and distinctive relationship to time. Only baseball can be called a "pastime." Baseball is above or outside time. Football, basketball, hockey, and soccer games are arbitrarily divided into measured quarters, halves, or periods. They are controlled, even dominated, by time. Not so of baseball, which either ignores time or dominates it. An inning theoretically can go on forever. The same is, of course, true of a game. Interruptions generally are limited to acts of God, such as darkness or rain, or to cultural and quasi-natural occurrences, such as curfew or midnight (in games played under the lights). If for some reason—dust in a batter's eye, rain, or the like—a baseball game must be halted, "time out" is not taken, with referees looking at their watches. Rather, time is "called" by the umpire. Again theoretically, time could be "called" and remain "called" forever.

Baseball is played in a unique spatial frame. Other games are played inside defined and limited areas: rectangular or near-rectangular fields, floors, or rinks. Not so with baseball. Baseball is played within the lines of a projection from home plate, starting from the point of a ninety-degree angle and extending to infinity. Were it not for the intervention of fences, buildings, mountains, and other obstacles in space, a baseball traveling within the ultimate projection of the first and third base lines could be fair, and full and infinitely in play. Baseballs never absolutely go out of bounds. They are either fair or foul; and even foul balls are, within limits, playable and are part of the game.

Baseball is distinguished from other games, also, in the way it is controlled by umpires. An umpire is very different from a referee, a field judge, or a linesman. Baseball uses umpires and no one else, an important distinction. And one umpire is always wholly responsible.

One occasionally hears the cry "Fire the referee," but one seldom hears "Kill the referee." That cry is reserved for umpires with good reason. Umpires have to be dealt with absolutely, for their power is absolute. Referees are men called or appointed. Umpires, by contrast, seem to exist by their own right and exercise undelegated power that is not to be reviewed. They are not asked to make judgments. They make them. The word itself carries this strength. It is derived from the Old French word *nompere*, meaning one who is alone or without a peer (literally, without a father or a superior). "Refuse not," the medieval divines warned, "the umpeership and judgments of the Holy Ghoste."

Baseball is different from other major sports in two other significant ways. First, the individual is under constant surveillance. At all times, one player, at least, is personally accountable. In football, a player may fall down and get up with mud all over him; and no one knows whether he has done his job. In basketball and in hockey, it is difficult to follow the action and measure the responsibility of each player.

Second, baseball is a game of records, team and individual. The bookkeeping is balanced. It shows earned runs and unearned runs. Hits are credited to batters and debited to pitchers. Errors are recorded along with assists and put-outs. Times at bat, home runs, triples, singles, sacrifices, strike-outs, passed balls, wild pitches, walks, balks, runs batted in, runs scored, and batting, fielding, and pitching averages all are in the book. The game is played for the game, but also for the record.

At the end of the last game of this year's World Series, one knew not only that the Yankees had won the series, but also that Reggie Jackson was the first man in history to hit five home runs in a series, and that he hit them in his last nine times at bat. Moreover, he hit four of them on his last four swings; and each of the last three was hit on the first pitch to him in that time at bat.

The game is the same whether played in the Astrodome, in Yankee Stadium, or as described by Robert Fitzgerald in his poem "Cobb Would Have Caught It":

> In sunburnt parks where Sundays lie,
> Or the wide wastes beyond the cities,
> Teams in grey deploy through sunlight.
>
> Talk it up, boys, a little practice.
> Coming in stubby and fast, the baseman
> Gathers a grounder in fat green grass.
> Picks it stinging and clipped as wit
> Into the leather: a swinging step
> Wings it deadeye down to first.
> Smack. Oh, atta boy, attaold boy.
>
> Catcher reverses his cap, pulls down
> Sweaty casque, and squats in the dust;
> Pitcher rubs new ball on his pants,
> Chewing, puts a jet behind him;
> Nods past batter, taking his time.
> Batter settles, tugs at his cap:
> A spinning ball: step and swing to it,
> Caught like a cheek before it ducks

Another Good Season

By shivery hickory: socko, baby:
Cleats dig into dust. Outfielder,
On his way, looking over shoulder,
Makes it a triple; A long peg home.

Innings and afternoons. Fly lost in sunset.
Throwing arm gone bad. There's your ball game.
Cool reek of the field. Reek of companions.

An Endangered Species: The Rural Mailbox

The most recently identified endangered species is not a bird or a beast, or a fish or a flower or a weed or a tree. It is not a relative of the snail darter or of the lousewort. It is not threatened by spreading suburbs, freeways, industrial growth, or by new dams or waterways recommended by the Army Corps of Engineers.

The endangered species is the traditional rural mailbox, and its mountings.

The threat was initiated by the Insurance Institute for Highway Safety and was quickly taken up and sustained by the United States Postal Service, thus providing another example of how some of the worst things done by government are initiated by private businesses, especially by institutes and corporations.

According to the reports, the Insurance Institute has discovered that the roadside rural free delivery mailboxes, together with their sustaining posts and mountings, are a threat to the life and limb of automobile drivers as well as to the automobile itself.

The Insurance Institute, modestly admitting that its data are "sketchy," nonetheless has published a "Status

44

Report," charging that the mailboxes are a serious road-side hazard.

The prime example, cited by the institute, is a recent case in Texas, in which a driver, reportedly swerving to avoid a motorcyclist on a narrow road, struck a row of mailboxes and was killed when one supporting post pierced the windshield and struck him.

To make matters worse, the Texas Transportation Institute, funded by the Federal Highway Administration, had conducted a test in which a multiple-box installation, not unlike the real thing in Texas, was struck by a car going sixty miles an hour (five miles above the national speed limit for major highways). In the test, the horizontal plank on which the boxes were fixed drove through the windshield, striking the test dummy. There was no reported test using the popular wagon-wheel multiple-box mounting.

The United States Postal Service, stung by the results of the Texas Transportation Department and stirred by the report of the Insurance Institute, is now looking into the whole matter in order to, as it asserts, "explore the possibility of establishing safety requirements for mailbox supports." Meanwhile, the Insurance Institute is continuing to sponsor research in the hope of developing safe mailbox and mounting designs.

The end result of both government and insurance companies' research, bureaucracies in action, is likely to be the same set of recommendations: First, a soft-plastic mailbox, rather than the traditional, standard U.S. Mail box, is likely to be prescribed.

Most certainly, there will be standard specifications as to the height and composition, as well as the shape, of the supporting post or structure and as to the color of boxes, a color scientifically determined not to attract the attention of any automobile drivers other than the mailman or -woman.

Cedar posts used in wet-land areas will be banned, as well as solid oak in temperate, reasonably high-ground installations, and solid locust, the only sure post in termite and dry-rot zones, will have to go. Cantilevered mountings will be illegal, as well as those on the frames of old walking ploughs. The welded chain support will be outlawed on at least two counts, the first that it distracts drivers and the second that despite its appearance, it is highly inflexible.

Boxes mounted on posts set in milk cans filled with cement, which, when knocked down by cars or snowplows or farm boys on the way home from school (this was in pre-school-bus days), could be set up again, may survive, in principle, if not in their original crude reality.

Boxes painted in any but the "official color," miniatures of the main house, or the barn, or even the country churches that they serve, will surely be forbidden, and the popular Uncle Sam holding the mailbox will be driven from the roadside.

Any and all of these things can happen, unless there is a counterstudy showing how many lives are saved because post-office boxes of various colors, shapes, and mountings along the road have warned persons driving in a fog, either of mist or of alcohol, as to where the roadside ended and the ditch began, or marked in snow-blown plains the line between the road and field, or how drivers alerted and forewarned by hitting mailboxes have been saved from worse fates, like running into ditches or hitting great trees or rocky banks.

As a spokesman for the Postal Service said, "I don't think anyone knows how large the problem might be."

God's in His World

The poet Robert Browning, in a moment of lyrical enthusiasm, wrote the often-quoted lines: "God's in His heaven/All's right with the world."

Not so today. Until recently, it was accepted that God might be resting quietly in His heaven and that the world was running reasonably well without Him. Within the last few years, however, his presence and power have been noted, if not invoked, to explain or justify earthly events and actions.

The first significant announcement of the involvement of God in a recent terrestrial decision was one made by President Ford. In the act of pardoning Nixon, Ford said that he was acting as "God's humble servant." I wonder why persons who assert that they are God's servants so often include the adjective "humble." The same persons, at other times in high office, tend to say that they are proud to be the chosen servants of the electorate. In any case, as God's servants they should operate without adjectival qualifications.

The second significant involvement of God in earthly events was announced by the Con Edison officials. In their first public statement after the New York blackout, they called that event "an act of God." After additional study, they admitted that mechanical and human failures contributed to God's failure.

In the same spirit, it was suggested that a recent flooding of a subway line in Washington, D.C., was not primarily an act of God, but that He was an accessory before the act. The explanation had to do with the way in which, on the third day, when the waters were separated from the dry land, God had not anticipated the subway and had not had the foresight to provide a different geological formation for the lower basin of the Potomac River.

God is not often given credit for positive achievements, but some politicians share time and responsibility, and occasionally credit, with the Deity. President Eisenhower, in prayer before going to sleep, reportedly asked God to look after the country while he, the President, was asleep. The President evidently was willing to bear the burdens and the credit of the day and to let God bear the burdens and the credit at night. President Carter says that he talks to Jesus and prays often, especially when he feels "a trepidation." He has not attempted to distinguish times or decisions in which the divine influence is to be given more or less credit.

There is also a negative theological force, which is generally not recognized in government: the role of the "Devil's advocate." George Ball played that role in opposing the war in Vietnam. Reportedly, George was set up to argue, time and time again, against Vietnam policy. Set against him were the defenders of the good cause, Dean Rusk and Robert McNamara. Evidently, George lost every argument, as the war was escalated and extended.

There is much to be said for the simple integrity of Flip Wilson's Geraldine, whose ultimate defense is "The Devil made me do it." That is less hypocritical than to imply that having won an argument with the Devil's advocate, one has proceeded in certainty and righteousness.

God is not to be mocked, says Saint Paul in his letter to the Galatians. Blaming God is not mocking, even though the blame may not be deserved. (It is unfair, and not offset by proper credit.) God would, I believe, rather be recognized, even to be blamed, than be mocked by being ignored.

In any case, the best judgment we can make is that of the poet Reed Whittemore, who concludes his poem on the seven days of creation with these lines:

There, then, was the world. The man surveyed it.
He doubted it was his duty to call it good.
He knew it to be but a world like any other.
He knew that his god, now resting, had made what he could.

Chrysler and Country: If Marx Had Known

If Karl Marx had known about the automobile, or anticipated the automobile culture of America, he might well have amended his theories in order to assert that the capitalistic system needs either war *or* the automobile industry (or both) to stimulate economic growth. There are clear points of similarity between the two as economic forces. They use essentially the same materials, principally fuel and metals. They both demand great supplies of manpower and a concentration of technological effort. Both consume great amounts of money and of credit. Total automobile credit outstanding in the United States at the end of 1978 was more than $88 billion. The defense budget of the federal government for that year was about $100 billion, and the federal budget deficit was about $49 billion.

There is also a disturbing similarity between the two, when defense expenditures support actual war, in their common propensity to maim and to kill people. During the months of high casualties in Vietnam, defenders of the war occasionally pointed out that more people had been killed in automobile accidents at home than had been killed in the war during the same period of time.

Marx noted that an extended and expensive war might eventually have a depressing and destructive effect on a capitalistic system. Obviously, today, the combined cost of maintaining a large military establishment, which is not only unproductive in economic terms but positively wasteful, and an excessively large and wasteful automobile culture is too much for the American economy to carry. We can no longer afford both our defense establishment and our automobile culture. What can be done about the first is a matter of politics. What can be done about the second is a matter of both politics and economics. According to a Hertz Corporation study published last summer, Americans are spending approximately $445 billion a year, more than one-fourth of national personal income, on automobiles. Making up five percent of the world's population, we own almost one-half of all passenger cars in the world, with one car for every 1.28 Americans. About fifteen percent of the world's annual production of petroleum is used each year to fuel American cars.

We have more cars and trucks than we need. We have a greater variety of cars than is necessary to satisfy reasonable consumer needs. Before World War II, making a choice of a car was relatively simple. Most cars had less than one-hundred-horsepower engines. There were only four or five models in each line. The models usually were called simply sedans, coaches, coupés. Now there are at least nine different kinds of Chevrolets. One can, if sufficiently agitated by the advertisements, spend a whole lifetime driving a Chevrolet and never be sure that one has the right kind.

Beyond makes and models, size and power, there are the special names of cars to be weighed before purchase. A prospective driver must consider his image, and ask questions such as: What is my totem animal? Am I a cougar, a pinto, a rabbit, a skylark, or a sky hawk? Or if one is into prestigious locales and watering spots, do I want to imagine myself in Capri, in Malibu, in Aspen, Versailles, or Monte Carlo? No company is offering a Coney Island or an Atlantic City. For those interested in astronomy, there is the modest choice of Nova, Vega, Comet, and Electra, and for those of tough fiber, there are the Matador, the Cutlass, the Maverick, the Renegade.

The Japanese manufacturers have stayed mostly with company names so far. We may expect, though, that in a future series, they will be offering, under the urging of American advertising consultants, Samurais, Kamikazes, Hara-kiris, etc. Our cars are too large and too heavy. Most are overpowered. With a national speed limit set at fifty-five miles an hour, auto manufacturers provide speedometers that will give readings from fifty percent to one hundred percent higher than the legal limit, and provide engines capable of propelling the car beyond the speed limit in comparable measure. It has been suggested that even if the engines and their power were adjusted to keep them within the legal range, the speedometers could remain the same. The last fifty miles on the speedometer could be like President Carter's lust: only for the imagination. Obviously, our automobiles consume too much fuel. They pollute too much. They kill and maim too many people. With no significant change in life style, but simply by driving cars of reasonable power and size, we could save as much as $100 billion a year in transportation costs.

In the midst of all this, the government has been asked

to guarantee a loan of $1.6 billion for the failing Chrysler Corporation. Both Houses of the Congress, the House of Representatives and the Senate, have responded positively to the request, supported by the Carter administration. Congressional debate on the proposal never got much beyond consideration of the narrow and immediate issues of loss of jobs, and of effects on communities, especially Detroit, that have Chrysler installations. The broader issues of the automobile and of American culture were never seriously discussed, nor was the more limited question of the condition of the automobile industry itself.

If these issues had been raised, the whole discussion might have used as its controlling text and rule of action that most-remembered utterance of Charlie Wilson, Secretary of Defense in the Eisenhower administration, following his career as president of General Motors. Wilson said, "I thought what was good for our country was good for General Motors, and vice versa." What Charlie Wilson would have said about the loan can only be guessed at, but if he had applied his 1950 judgment about the common and inseparable interests of the United States and of General Motors, he might well have reasoned as follows.

First, that the loan to Chrysler will not be good for the country because it will keep an inefficient producer in operation. On the other hand, it will be good for General Motors since the loan, by keeping the inefficient Chrysler company in business, will make it possible for General Motors to make profits and control the American automobile market without great difficulty, and without attracting too much attention from the antitrust people. This conclusion would not have wholly satisfied the demands of his principle.

Charlie might then have moved on to consider the

effect of offering the loan guarantee to Ford Motor Company instead. Ford reports that it is losing $1 billion a year on its car and truck production and sales in the United States and Canada. A loan guarantee for Ford would make Ford more competitive with General Motors, which would be good for the country, thus meeting one-half of Wilson's standard of public good. But it would not be good for General Motors, thus failing to meet the requirements of the other half of the Wilson rule.

Charlie might then have concluded that the best arrangement of all would be to provide help neither to Chrysler nor to Ford, but to General Motors, to help move that company to produce the kinds of cars that the country needs and should have, and also to make General Motors more competitive with foreign automobile manufacturers, who are taking over more and more of the American automobile industry and the American automobile market.

Old "Engine Charlie" may well have spoken with the voice of a prophet twenty years ago. What would be good for General Motors could be good for the country and "vice versa."

Moving on Schedule

Those unhappy with the response of Congress to current problems, such as inflation and energy shortages, may have their spirits lifted by a quick look at some of its long-range interests and concerns.

The long-term view is a departure, possibly a great leap forward, from actions of recent Congresses. While overlooking or postponing action on contemporary matters, it looked to the righting of injustices of the past. In that spirit, it restored citizenship to Robert E. Lee; and promoted George Washington to General of the Armies of the United States.

Some American citizens are concerned about any weakening of our attitude of disapproval and nonrecognition of Cuba and our denial of most-favored-nation treatment in trade with that nation. They can rest more easily, knowing a bill has been introduced in the House to ban any importation of citrus and tropical fruits or winter vegetables from Cuba until after 1989.

The 1989 date is a little short of our accepted period of denying recognition or regular trade following an international dispute. In the case of Germany and Japan, following our victory over them in World War II, recognition and resumption of trade followed almost immediately. In the case of China, however, there was a thirty-year period between the time of our disappointment and the resumption of diplomatic and trade relationships.

If the thirty-year rule is applied to Cuba, such recognition should not occur until 1991, or approximately two years after the 1989 date set by the House bill. Vietnam will have to wait, by this standard, until the year 2003.

For those who think that the Constitution of the United States is in need of greater recognition and respect, there should be comfort in the fact that a bill has been introduced in the Senate that would make September 17, 1987, and every September 17 thereafter a legal holiday known as Constitution Day. The reason for the delay until 1987 is not quite clear, although it undoubtedly is related to the time of the drafting of the document.

A synthetic-fuels bill introduced in the House would provide two million barrels of synthetic fuel per day by 1990, only eleven years away. Another bill eventually would replace ten percent or more of the gasoline used in the United States with alcohol and other fuels.

For those worried about the federal budget and government spending, there should be consolation and assurances in a House resolution which provides that federal budget outlays after September 30, 1985, shall not exceed twenty percent of the gross national product of the preceding fiscal year, except in the event of war or economic necessity as determined and declared by the Congress.

According to the testimony of Henry Kissinger on the SALT II treaty, our Minuteman missiles will not become vulnerable to Soviet counterforce strikes until after 1985. This gives us six years of relative security.

There is the further assurance that scheduled increases in the tax rate for Social Security will level off at 7.65 percent of payroll by 1990.

If one accepts the findings of historians, astronomers, and students of the Bible that Christ was actually born eight years earlier than has been believed, the second millennium will not end in the year 2000, but rather in the year 1992. If this fact is recognized, the dates for all of the above-scheduled good and bad things will have to be changed. It may be eight years later than we think.

Embarking
and Disembarking

Recently, it was announced that the army is planning a Rapid Deployment Force of about 110,000 troops, including the Eighty-second Airborne Division. The force will also include units from the air force, the navy, and the marines. It will be on call for crises outside Europe.

Plans for the new force resulted partly from a secret "consolidated guidance" that civilian Pentagon officials issued to the armed services last year. It is not clear just what consolidated guidance is, nor how it can be distinguished from "unconsolidated guidance" or "nonconsolidated guidance" or "random guidance."

The new force (which was initially called the Unilateral Corps) will be completely under United States control. Once established, its troops will not be diverted to NATO use, even if an emergency develops in the NATO area. The force is said to be the army's answer to President Carter's desire for a specialized force for conflicts in the Third World. Evidently the force will not be used in the First or Second Worlds, although Alexander Haig, the recently retired NATO commander, has said that it will be a "go-anywhere force."

The unit will be available to the "unified commanders."

The Commander-in-Chief for the Pacific, for example, could call upon it for help instead of having to find and round up available small units. The Rapid Deployment Force apparently will be prepared to fight "half-wars." This capacity was identified by Robert McNamara, Lyndon Johnson's Secretary of Defense, when McNamara said that the United States was prepared to fight two and one-half wars: total nuclear, total conventional, and a half-war such as he planned for Vietnam.

There is, we have been assured by the State Department, no decision to deploy the yet-unformed force, although State says it is aware of contingency planning. The army will not keep the entire force in one place, awaiting crises; rather, it will equip all components so that they can respond quickly and as a unit.

Although it is reported that the established military forces of the country are understaffed and underpowered, military spokesmen warn those concerned that they ought not consider the unit a new addition to U.S. striking power. The military will form the Rapid Deployment Force with available troops, and will work around current shortages of ships and transportation to move military units and weapons to distant points when needed.

The Arabs have been assured by columnist Charles Bartlett, who favors establishing the force, that it is "no threat to Arab sovereignty." Bartlett has concluded that although the force seems to have no clear mission, it will be worth its cost "if only to counteract perceptions of this nation as a supine giant."

Much of this sounds like a rerun, a carry-over, or a carry-back to the Defense Department of Robert McNamara, to the era of unification, contingency plans, systems and analyses, half-wars, and Special Forces.

Why not just bring back the marines? They were a unified force, a unilateral force, a "go-anywhere" force, from the halls of Montezuma to the shores of Tripoli, a quick-strike force. The country and the world always knew when the marines had landed, and why.

The restoration of the Marine Corps to its traditional role would immediately do more for the national image and spirit, do more to show that the United States is not a "supine giant," than will a Rapid Deployment Force produced as a result of a "consolidated guidance."

How We Can Win
in the Survival Game

In 1960, the words "strategy" and "strategic" carried traditional meanings. Both applied to planning and actions. But by 1967, a change had taken place. That year, the Johnson administration approached the Soviet Union on the possibility of holding talks on "Strategic Arms Limitations." The weapons now defined the purposes.

By 1974, nuclear-weapons thinkers had begun to talk about "strategic superiority" as some kind of quantitative measure of nuclear advantage. I did not quite understand what was meant by the term in 1974, nor did I fully understand Secretary of Defense Harold Brown later, when he described "meaningful nuclear superiority" as a "disparity in strategic capability," which can be "translated into political effect."

I was consoled in my lack of comprehension by the fact that in 1974, Henry Kissinger, when asked what was meant by the term, responded by saying, "What in God's name is strategic superiority? What can you do with it?"

If Kissinger didn't know what the words meant, possibly no one knew, or needed to know. Thus I reassured myself for five years, until the recent SALT II hearings.

For the same Henry Kissinger, in his testimony on the

treaty, said that his 1974 words had been spoken under stress, or in a moment of pique, and that he did in fact in 1974 know, and does now know, what constitutes "strategic superiority."

Kissinger observes a "perilous momentum" in favor of the Russians, but whether this is a "pure momentum," or a "momentum of their potential," such as was identified by Secretary of Defense Melvin Laird in the Nixon administration, he does not say.

Whatever kind of momentum it is, Kissinger says it is developing "ominously" against the United States. According to some estimates, the United States now has enough nuclear warheads to kill all of the Russians (or at least all of the important ones) approximately fifty times, and the Russians can kill all of the important Americans twenty-two times. We thus have a "strategic superiority" in a ratio of 5.0 to 2.2. By the year 1985, if SALT II is ratified and implemented, the ratio will be 6.0 to 6.0, with Russians and Americans able to kill each other sixty times. This is called Mutual Assured Destruction, or MAD times sixty.

That prospect calls for thinking outside the established lines and patterns of thought about "strategic superiority." It demands "zero-based thinking," a method of thinking comparable to the accounting method used in the currently popular "zero-based budgeting."

Zero-based thinking about nuclear weapons must start with the assumption that MAD has already been achieved by both sides. It must seek, at that point, to answer the question of which nation has what I will call the best MSP (Minimal Survival Potential).

Obviously, the nation with the greatest MSP will have "strategic superiority." The United States has three principal MSP advantages.

The first is our readiness for evacuation. We evacuate about thirty percent of the population of major urban areas to the suburbs five days a week, about fifty percent on weekends, and two-thirds on special holidays, leaving in the central cities principally only the lame, the old, and the poor.

In anticipation of a nuclear exchange, and in order to upgrade the value of our normal evacuation potential, the President should be given, in the name of national defense, authority to move holidays. Thus, he could advance, say, Memorial Day to April 1, or the Fourth of July to June 15, with the understanding that when the advanced date was announced, people would accept the announcement as a signal that they should do on the advancement date exactly what they had planned to do on the regular holiday date. The movable holiday—the MH—could be "strategically" the "rough equivalent" to the MX missile system.

Our second advantage is in our heavily armed citizenry. It is estimated that there are in possession of U.S. citizens, protected by the Second Amendment to the Constitution and by the National Rifle Association, approximately one hundred million guns of various kinds, together with an adequate supply of ammunition. Russian citizens, on the other hand, are not so armed. Occupation of the United States, even after saturation bombing, would be a high-risk venture, as citizens with their guns would come down from the hills and rise from the rubble. Consider how much more difficult the Russian invasion of Hungary and Czechoslovakia would have been if the Hungarians and the Czechs had possessed guns and ammunition as Americans do.

Our third advantage, a growing one, was pointed out to me by a student product of the 1960s, who observed that the movement in the United States to provide more and better facilities for the handicapped—such things as ramps instead of steps, hydraulic lifts for entrance to buses and trains, heat-activated elevators, modified automobiles, changed industrial processes, and so forth—could, if carried far enough, add greatly to our "strategic superiority" and MSP capacity. All of these changes, he noted, would be helpful when those maimed by the great nuclear exchange (designated in nuclear war language as "dilatory" or "delayed" fatalities rather than as "prompt fatalities") would be able to launch a "final strike," and also begin putting civilization back together. He went on to suggest that the modifications being made in the name of helping the handicapped might be carried further in anticipation of the time when only mutants were left in charge.

It is quite possible, if zero-based thinking is followed, that in SALT II, assuming that MAD is not attempted and that we get by the "window of peril" recently identified by Kissinger, the discussion and controversy will not be over cruise missiles or neutron bombs or laser rays, as is now anticipated, but rather over assurances of fixed holidays and early warnings of changed dates, over parity of equality in citizens' possession of arms (this could be a strong point for the United States to make in the name of human rights), and, finally, over limitations and verification of programs and projects to aid the handicapped and mutilated, and over preparations for the Age of Mutants.

For the Want of Horses

We must take a new look at the cavalry, its traditional role and future possibilities in international military power, if any progress is to be made toward world peace and stability. A mounted military might be far more civilized than what we now have, and less dangerous to us.

The story of the horsed cavalry goes back almost to the beginning of the history of war. When Job wrote of the horse, "He saith among the trumpets, Ha, ha: and he smelleth the battle afar off, the thunder of the captains, and the shouting," he was not referring to the cavalry horse of later times; for the horse of Biblical times was too small and light to carry an armed man. The horse was then used as a draft animal—to haul supplies and, more nobly, to pull war chariots into battle.

Later, with greater strength, the horse became the mount of the cavalryman and of the knight. The earliest-known cavalry was that of the Persians. As a fighting unit, it accepted only riders of noble birth. On down through the centuries, as long as the supply of nobility lasted, the cavalry was their haven.

The first serious challenge to nobility as the sustaining characteristic of the cavalryman came, as one might expect, from Oliver Cromwell and the Puritans. Cromwell noted that he had in his army few potential horsemen of noble birth, few gentlemen's sons or persons of quality, but rather a lot of "decayed servingmen and tapsters and such kind of fellows." He set out to establish religious conviction and trust in a leader as substitutes for birth and noble tradition in inspiring heroic military action, particularly by the cavalry. He also abolished the spectacular cavalry charge at the gallop; his horsemen came on with Puritan restraint, at a "pretty round trot."

The cavalry was set back, as was culture, by the Puritan intervention. But it made a comeback, as did the Church of England and the monarchy, and held its place firmly for 210 years. Then it was downgraded, both as to tactics and as to source of manpower, during the American Civil War. (Civil wars are bad for institutions.)

In the course of its long history, the cavalry has carried out functions similar to those of major military institutions, excepting the navy, the pure infantry, and missile-delivered bombs. The heavy cavalry, known as cuirassiers, with heavy horses carrying big men, were the equivalents of modern tanks. The light cavalry, commonly called hussars, were used like airplanes in World War I—for reconnaissance, occasionally as support units in battle, and for raids behind the lines. The third type of cavalry, the dragoons, were basically soldiers who used their horses as Jeeps or personnel carriers for transport to suitable battlefield positions, from which they fought on foot.

Through the centuries, cavalries have been the objects of extensive tactical and strategic theorizing. Experts have debated formations, weapons, time and velocity of the charges, uniforms, nationality of riders, and breeding of horses.

In the armies of most countries of the world today, the cavalry has been abandoned. The British retain the Life Guards and the Blues for ceremonial purposes only, although it must be said for the British that they did not easily give up the horse units. As late as 1927, the British defense budget reported £607,000 for forage and £72,000 for petrol. In 1933, when the German tank divisions were being built up, the British still had twenty-one horse regiments in the regular army, sixteen in the territorial army, and twenty-one in the Indian army.

And in 1936, the British Secretary of State for War apologized when he announced that he had decided to mechanize eight cavalry regiments. "It is like," he said, "asking a great musical performer to throw away his violin and devote himself in the future to the Gramophone." That action may have marked the end of an era, wrote the cavalry historian James D. Lunt, and may even have marked "the time when man began his headlong slide down the slope to self-destruction."

The United States today has twenty-six horses in the whole defense establishment, and they are used only for state funerals. The horse-drawn caissons were saved by action of Congress some ten years ago, in the face of Defense Department arguments that hearses were cheaper than horses. The Turks still have some cavalry units; the Chinese, it is believed, in Mongolia; and the Russians, it is suspected, somewhere.

It is not too late to try to re-establish the cavalry in all the armies of the world. Bringing the cavalry back would accomplish many good things. The cavalry would attract frustrated potential polo players who might otherwise go into the CIA. Conditioning, feeding, and grooming would occupy much of the time of the colonels and junior officers, thus keeping them from drawing contingency plans for wars of various kinds.

The cavalry's return could even break the stalemate in arms limitation and disarmament talks, for it would introduce new standards and a new vocabulary for measuring comparative strength of rival military forces. Power could be measured in rough equivalence of cavalry units. We could trade off, for example, one B-1 bomber for one thousand units of cavalry—and thus gradually shift away from talk of disarmament to rearmament, but with the weapons of earlier wars.

In fact, we might proceed unilaterally to build up our horses forces. In the event that the Russians, who are suspected of having at least three thousand cavalrymen and horses, should come by horse, we could meet them on their own terms.

The economic fallout would benefit saddle-makers, blacksmiths, and producers of oats and hay.

Old Counselors May Fade, but Not Away

The role of counselors is exceedingly subtle, as Chester Cooper reports in a recent *New Republic* article.

According to Mr. Cooper, in June of 1968, Vice-President Humphrey was ready to give a speech advocating an immediate and total halt of the bombing of North Vietnam. Before giving the speech, the Vice-President or his advisers decided to consult with two established counselors, Averell Harriman and Cyrus Vance, who at the time were in Paris in peace negotiations with the North Vietnamese.

The counselors, we are told by Mr. Cooper, both favored a bombing halt and a cease fire. Yet, they refused to endorse the Humphrey decision for fear that it might move President Johnson to resist a bombing-halt proposal that their staff was preparing. They were also concerned that if the negotiations failed following the delivery of the speech, Johnson might claim that the speech had contributed to the failure.

The counselors gave counsel. They kept secret their opposition to the bombing. The speech was not given. The negotiations failed.

The counselors survived. One remains a counselor. The other is Secretary of State.

The counselor is as old as the history of government. Roman emperors, medieval princes, and later kings all used counselors, either for help and guidance or as excuses for mistakes of judgment.

Counselors of the past were identified as persons. The depersonalized, institutionalized counselor is an American contribution to statecraft and diplomacy. It should be credited more to the Democratic party and its Presidential administrations than to the Republicans.

The counselors as a body were not recognized and identified as such in the Roosevelt administration; but it was in that administration that they took root. They were, as one might say, the legacy of that administration. They appear and reappear in Democratic administrations as needed—and sometimes even when not needed.

The general line of succession is from the Roosevelt administration, from the twelve who knew the Master. Some, like Averell Harriman, were given diplomatic missions. Some served as junior advisers or legal counsel. Starting with the Truman administration, Clark Clifford ranked high among the lawyer-counselors.

After leaving government, the counselors generally established or became part of important law firms, engaged in international law and high-level lobbying, euphemistically referred to as "representing the people before governmental agencies." Others, because they were not lawyers or for other reasons, found refuge in various foundations and institutes during their out-of-power periods. McGeorge Bundy, of the Kennedy and Johnson administrations, followed this tradition when he became president of the Ford Foundation. Charles Schultze, budget director in the Johnson administration, found refuge in the Brookings Institution during the Nixon years, then returned to power with the Carter administration.

Out of power, the counselors surface as authors of articles, usually printed in *Foreign Affairs*, on subjects like the bearing of the Kellogg-Briand peace pact on SALT II. Or they appear as members of various commissions and committees, such as the Trilateral Commission and the Committee on the Present Danger.

In law firms and institutions, some counselors wait, like Cincinnatus, plowing the front forty so as not to miss the messenger calling them back to the service of the Republic.

When they are called back, it is usually for relatively short duty. Sometimes they are asked to negotiate peace settlements, often of wars that they have advocated, as in the case of Vance and Harriman in Paris in the summer of 1968. Sometimes they are asked to serve as cabinet members for a full term (as it appears Vance is now serving), but more commonly for short periods and in emergencies, as was the case when President Johnson made Clark Clifford his Secretary of Defense.

Old counselors—unlike the old soldiers described by General Douglas MacArthur—do not fade away. They fade, but not quite away. They have the vitality of the lower forms of plant life. Like moss on a rock, they are never more than slightly green when they are at the high point of their vitality. They fade to a winter gray, only to return to the gray-green of their summer. As Robert Lowell said of the Republicans and of the poor in Maine, they "cannot sink and will not swim."

Beyond Thorstein Veblen

A few weeks ago, I met a young Saudi Arabian. Our talk (this was before the Afghanistan crisis) turned to oil, but not to production levels, prices, or possible invasion of the Middle East by either Russia or the United States in order to secure essential oil supplies. Rather, we spoke of ways and means of reducing the demand for Middle East oil, especially by the United States. The burden, the young man pointed out, is especially heavy for his country, because whenever other countries cut back production for any reason, the burden of making up the shortage falls on Saudi Arabia.

As a result of the Iranian revolution, for example, Saudi Arabian production went up to 10.4 million barrels per day and then settled back to 9.5 million barrels per day, a level one million barrels higher than Saudi Arabia wished to supply.

The young Saudi listed the following reasons why his country wanted to reduce its production and sales: the immediate effects of inflation, unnecessary and inadequately planned urbanization, the inflow of foreigners, corruption, maldistribution of wealth, social unrest. He noted also the long-range disadvantages of rapid and excessive oil production by his country: eventual exhaustion of supplies and unsound investment of oil revenues, with the possibility that such investments might be destroyed by inflation or by expropriation in the country in which they had been made. He preferred, he said, to have oil in the ground in Saudi Arabia rather than bank deposits in Switzerland, corporate stocks and bonds, or even real property like land in Iowa.

Despite price rises, urgings from the President, and corporate advertising to encourage conservation, Americans' demand for oil and gasoline continued to rise in 1979.

We continue to be the greatest consumers, if not the greatest overconsumers, in the history of the world. With about five percent of the world's population, we consume about one-third of the world's annual production of fuel. We own almost one-half of all the passenger cars in the world, with one car for every 1.28 persons. In 1975, ten percent of our material production was directed and used for the construction and maintenance of automobiles, and fifteen percent of the world's annual production of petroleum was used to fuel them.

According to a report by the Environmental Protection Agency several years ago, approximately twenty-eight tons of material from mines, fields, forests, and oceans were consumed each year per person in the United States. The overall annual consumption of material resources by the United States was more than twice that of Western Europe, four times that of Eastern Europe, and could not even be realistically compared with consumption in many other countries of the world. In some of those countries, people could live better on the waste of America, if it could be transported to them, than they now live.

Americans are overfed, overtransported, overfueled, overheated, overcooled, and overdefended. Some are overhoused. We are overpackaged and overadvertised, among other things. Conspicuous waste beyond the imagination of Thorstein Veblen has become a mark of American life.

This need not be the mark of our nation. America was not always an overconsuming and wasteful country. Well into the twentieth century, we were a frugal nation. Little fuel was used in agriculture. Horses were a major source of work-power, and they were sustained by the land on which they worked. Workers and their families lived near their work, in contrast with the situation today in which the average distance between home and work in the United States is estimated at fifteen miles.

There was some agricultural exploitation, but reasonable cycles of crop rotation with natural fertilization was the rule. Small-town living, and even city dwelling, did not allow for excessive waste. The six-pack, the throwaway bottle, and the plastic garbage bag had not yet been invented. Restraint during those years was not altogether a manifestation of virtue, although virtue was present. Necessity was a strong force.

Today, the force of necessity is, especially with reference to gasoline and oil, strong. The real test, however, is one of virtue of the kind that John Adams called forth from the inhabitants of the American colonies in 1776 as a price of political freedom. "We must," said Adams, "change our habits, our prejudices, our palates, our taste in dress, furniture, equipage [it was horses and carriages then, it is automobiles today], architecture." He reassured the colonists that, if they did this, they could "live and be happy."

Debt-Ceiling Time
in the Valley

Early October is debt-ceiling time in the Congress—time for passage of the annual King Canute resolution. This annual ritual has become something like the resolution of an alcoholic. Each year, as the habit becomes more positively fixed, the resolve of the addict becomes firmer.

This year, it was the Republicans' turn to worry publicly and to grieve over such facts as: There is approximately $3,100 of federal debt for every American and more than $100 billion of the debt is held by foreigners. The Democrats could counter by saying that seven years ago, when the Republicans were established in office, the per-capita debt was only $1,825 per American and that most of the $100 billion of debt held by foreigners was accumulated during the Nixon-Ford administration.

Republicans have no right to enjoy the debt-ceiling resolution debate. Rather, they deserve to suffer from it more than the Democrats. The debt ceiling more or less happened by accident, when Liberty Bond sales were authorized in 1917. But the Republicans conceived the idea of the temporary debt ceiling, as distinguished from the permanent ceiling.

The temporary debt ceiling was introduced during the Eisenhower administration. From that time forward, it has been much easier to raise the debt ceiling, since it has been viewed as merely temporary—not permanent or eternal. Thus, the permanent ceiling in 1955 was held at $275 billion, the level established in 1947; but the temporary ceiling was set at $281 billion. In 1959, the permanent ceiling was raised to $288 billion, and the temporary to $290 billion. In 1960, the last year of the Eisenhower administration, also an election year, fiscal restraint reasserted itself when the permanent ceiling was reduced to $285 billion. But the temporary ceiling was raised to $295 billion. This left the country with a permanent ceiling that was $3 billion less than in the previous year, and a temporary ceiling that was $5 billion higher than in the previous year.

In subsequent years, the permanent ceiling has never caught up with the temporary ceiling, except for short periods, usually following the April 15 collection of income taxes.

In neither Republican nor Democratic administrations have congressional debt-ceiling resolutions been effective in stopping the increase in the national debt. During the Kennedy and Johnson administrations, the permanent debt ceiling rose from $285 billion to $358 billion. The temporary increases during those years ranged from $8 billion in one year to $51 billion in another.

During the Nixon-Ford years, the permanent limit was raised from $358 billion to $400 billion. Last year, a temporary limit of $300 billion, added to the permanent limit, made a total of $700 billion.

The Carter administration proposed to continue the permanent ceiling at $400 billion, but to increase the temporary ceiling by $375 billion—for a high of $775 billion. The amount finally agreed upon, in a bill recently signed by the President, was $752 billion.

Obviously, the debt-ceiling resolution has done little, over the long run, to inhibit the increase in government spending or national debt. But it has forced the government into wasteful short-term financing practices, as the Treasury has tried to stay within the ceilings imposed by Congress.

But all is not lost. There is always the political diversion of the debates on the debt-ceiling resolution. The out party can enjoy the sport of pointing to the contradiction between word and performance on the part of the ins. The outs can promise that in their time, a time that is coming, the budget will be balanced and there will be a surplus with which the national debt, temporary and permanent, will be reduced. Possibly in the millennial year 2000—when the arms ceilings will be reached, the poverty program will be successful, the energy crisis will be over, and the lion will lie down with the lamb.

Is Justice Deaf?
Not Blind?

Most disturbing news: the Supreme Court has announced that it is considering the construction of a new building, a larger one with more space for staff, records, and whatever else the Supreme Court of the last quarter of the twentieth century may need. It has been suggested that the old building be used as a museum.

One must ask: What will the new court building be like?

One can fairly assume that it will be equipped with the latest technological aids for judges. For example, the new court could have adaptable chairs behind the bench. Each chair could be lowered or raised, as the justice wished, or could be hydraulically lifted from a lower chamber through the floor to the courtroom, with a sitting judge already seated, composed, and ready to judge. A justice who wished to leave the chamber might push a button and disappear, quietly and quickly, below the level of the bench.

The shape of the bench, too, might be changeable. Thus, for some cases, the justices might sit in a straight line. This was the shape of the bench until recently, when it was changed to something short of a half-circle. One explanation for the change was that justices were interrupting each other because one could not see when another was talking. The great principle that "Justice is blind" seems to be contradicted by this observation. Perhaps the inscription on the new building should read, JUSTICE IS DEAF. Instead of the blindfolded figure of Justice holding the scales, which stands outside the entrance to the court building today, the new court could be graced by a figure with a hearing aid.

For some cases, the half-circle or limited-arc bench could be used. In others, the bench might take the form of a V.

It might be possible, under the control of the Chief Justice, to change the shape of the bench during hearings, having all the justices move in on a person arguing before the Court at critical times, and then having the justices recede. The bench would thus have some of the same flexibility now built into theater and television stages. There could be changes in lighting as well.

The relationship of the Court to the Congress and the executive branch might well be taken into account, both in construction of the new court building and in its placement relative to the Capitol and the White House. The triangular relationship is a possibility, although the relationship is not quite that precise. The branches of the American government are not a trinity of equals. Moreover, the relationship of the Court to the Senate, at least in the procedure by which its members are chosen, is different from its relationship to the House.

With more space, more staff, and greater detachment, the Court might be tempted, as the Congress has been, to duplicate executive activities and responsibilities. The

Court might set up its own subcommittee on the federal budget. It might feel a need for its own intelligence agency and secret investigative unit. It might set up a special subcommittee on constitutional amendments, to study what the Congress is doing about amending the Constitution. It might even begin to make legislative recommendations, beyond those which the Chief Justice occasionally makes today, on Court needs and procedures.

The possibilities of an ever-expanding Court are, as the word suggests, unlimited.

There is, however, another course of action open to the Court. It could abandon the current building, letting it become a museum, and return to its old quarters in the Capitol, thereby making the first serious challenge to Parkinson's law. This move would also place the Court physically where it belongs constitutionally: slightly on the Senate's side of the Capitol, but closer to the Congress than it is to the executive branch. It would be closer to those who represent the people, and protected from the executive branch in the event that a President might be moved to pack or unpack the Court.

With less space for records and staff, a limitation dictated by space, the Court would have a strong defense against having to take cases such as some of those on which it has ruled recently. It could restrict its judgments to matters of greater legal, constitutional, and historical significance. With fewer decisions—whether those decisions be good or bad—the opinions, which in the long run may have more effect on the life of the nation, would almost certainly be better.

Blueberry-Muffin Mix, the Ultimate Indicator

Predictions of the depth and duration of the current recession, which will become a depression when it bottoms out, have consistently been in error. It is obvious that the indicators being used to measure and interpret economic change are either inadequate in themselves or are being badly read and interpreted. Yet, economists, business analysts, investment advisers, bankers, and other experts go on watching the changes in gross national product, personal income, installment credit, corporate profits, unemployment numbers, housing starts, inventories, capital investment, and so forth, and ignoring more subtle and proven indicators of economic change, some of which surprisingly rise during recession and fall during periods of prosperity.

One of the most reliable indicators (one that has been ignored by the experts) of short-range economic change, as well as of long-range trends, is, according to a grocery salesman I know, the sale of blueberry-muffin mix. In periods of rising optimism and expectations, and prosperity, these sales rise noticeably and remain at a high level. A downturn is shown by a falling off of blueberry-muffin-mix sales. According to this same astute salesman, oatmeal sales are an unreliable, even useless, indicator of economic conditions, as these sales remain relatively constant throughout the whole cycle of business change. His explanation for this stability is that whereas during recession, the less affluent in our society eat less and therefore buy less oatmeal, those losses are offset by the increased purchase of oatmeal by people whose income is declining, and who are consequently moving down from high- or middle-income consumption levels to the oatmeal level. The Department of Commerce does not include blueberry-muffin-mix sales in its economic-indicators report.

Among the indicators that rise during recession are three important ones: sales of Chinese checkers games, of jigsaw puzzles, and of Ouija boards. All of these demonstrated their reliability as measures of economic conditions during the Great Depression. Because of the distraction of television, and reports that the unemployed in the country spend much of their time watching the tube, these indicators will not show trends quite as clearly as they did before television. Nonetheless, they are worth watching.

With depression and unemployment come anxiety and restlessness. Chinese checkers is a game that takes a long time to play. It requires less concentration than does regular checkers. The outcome is left essentially to chance. The conditions of the game are not very different from those existing in a receding or depressed economy.

Working jigsaw puzzles is much like playing Chinese checkers. Much time is used. There is no serious interperson competition involved. Finishing a jigsaw puzzle is satisfying. A complete puzzle makes order out of chaos. The person who completes a puzzle has the temporary satisfaction of having put something in order and may sleep better for the achievement. Chaos may return in the morning.

More significant than Chinese checkers or jigsaw puzzles were the sales of Ouija boards during the Depression of the thirties. Such sales were not so much valuable as a general indicator of economic conditions, or as a measure of the quantitative aspects of the times, as they were as a measure of psychological attitudes, of anxiety and near despair.

A minor indicator in the thirties was the production and sales of the Target Cigarette Rolling Machine. With the machine, a smoker could roll his own cigarettes, reportedly saving a few cents a package. The savings were not as important as was the satisfaction of having manufactured something.

These old and tested indicators probably could not be wholly substituted for the more modern scientific standards now being used with mixed results, but if introduced subtly into what is called the "mix of measurements," they might be helpful to the economic prognosticators as they attempt to read the American economy and make their predictions.

We're Changing Eras
Almost as Often
as We Change Clothing

Who's got the era?

It is becoming more and more difficult to keep up with the coming and going of eras, and with their multiplicity, to say nothing of their significance.

I had scarcely adjusted to the new era announced after the launching of the first Sputnik in 1957, and was eagerly searching for the new philosophy, the new theology, and the new economic, social, and political forms that era was said to require, when I was told that a new era of science had been introduced with progress in nuclear biology.

In this new era, it was said, the nature of man itself might change. If that happened, depending on what direction the change took, there would be uncertainty as to whether new ideas and new social and cultural forms would be necessary, or whether the old ones (which I had come to believe had to be changed because of Sputnik) might again be relevant.

Era-changing is not limited to the field of science. It is occurring in foreign affairs and in world politics. Thus, in an article published in the *Wall Street Journal*, Irving Kristol announced the "end of an era." "Since Vietnam," Kristol said, "our foreign policy has collapsed into what can only be called a decadent Wilsonianism, retaining shreds and tatters of the traditional evangelical moralism and self-hypnotic legalism, but also displaying . . . new pathological features."

I had scarcely become reconciled to the end of this era, when I was informed by the press and the White House that with the recognition of China, a new era in international relations had been initiated. Zbigniew Brzezinski takes credit for ushering in this new era, if not escorting it or driving it in. Apparently, it is a part of the "new world order" that he has envisioned, an order that will be "architectural."

It also has been noted that the thinking underlying the new era is global, rather than regional, provincial, or historical. James Schlesinger, in discussing the development of oil and gas resources in Alaska, observed that those resources would be developed only in such a way as not to injure the "lower forty-eight states." Why he left out Hawaii, he did not explain. Possibly, it was not within the range of longitude within which his global thinking was then directed.

Words like "tangential" and "parabolic," "quadrants," "perimeters," "parameters," and "equations" are becoming more common. One sees reference to "the upper-left quadrant of the Western Hemisphere" and the "western half of the Southern Hemisphere." There are also more limited geometric applications, such as *Time* magazine's reference to the Middle East as the "Crisis Crescent," also referred to by the architecturally minded Brzezinski as the "arc of crisis."

And, of course, over all else, we are seeking—through both disarmament and armaments—a "global arms balance."

Aristotle would not have liked the new era. He believed in history and in philosophy. He probably would have preferred Henry Kissinger (who acknowledged that there were in his approach to foreign policy elements of Metternich, Kant, and Spinoza) over Brzezinski.

Aristotle warned against the dangers of the architectural approach to statecraft, as he saw those dangers in the proposals of Hippodamus, the first urban architect to turn to politics. "There is," Aristotle observed, "surely great confusion in all this." Much as President Carter said, in responding to a recent query about Taiwan, "The multiplicity of responsibility that a President has—the same issues that our nation has to face, I think, cause some lack of central focus quite often."

Beyond J. Edgar

In the ABSCAM project, the FBI, operating under a new director of no reputation, has come out of the closet. It has begun to serve "the law," which gives the bureau authority and responsibility not only to detect crime, to pursue and capture criminals, but also to *prevent* crime. This latter purpose is at once the basic justification for ABSCAM and the bureaucratic dynamic that generated it.

The critical point is not whether or not the ABSCAM actions legally involved "entrapment," but that a government agency charged with crime control set up conditions that would move persons to perform illegal acts, following which they would be prosecuted. In defense of its activities, the FBI has said that the persons who were offered "bribes" were not "targets," i.e., picked as victims by the bureau, nor were they selected at random. They had been named by an informer, who, seeking to reduce his sentence in a stolen-property case, named politicians who either had taken bribes or who might be tempted. Evidently, the FBI, claiming that "scam" operations involving truck hijackings and fencing of stolen goods have discouraged these illegal activities, believes that through operations such as ABSCAM, political corruption and white-collar crime also will be discouraged.

The possibilities are almost without limit. Anyone subject to temptation would be fair game. The FBI could infiltrate the H. & R. Block Company, for example, and offer unsuspecting clients clever ways of avoiding payment of income taxes. The ten most-wanted persons could be determined in advance, moved to perform criminal action, and arrested immediately. There would then be no waiting list, nor embarrassment as the number wanted, but not caught, continued to grow.

It is in the business of purifying politics that the new technique has the greatest potential, though. That process is already well under way and has progressed at least partially through two stages. First was the effort to protect candidates from the electorate by limiting campaign contributions and requiring the disclosure of the names of contributors. In the ultimate purification, the government will finance all campaigns itself. That would leave only one serious question: Who or what agency will decide which candidate and which party will get the government money?

The second stage of purification is protecting the officeholder from his constituency through such devices as open committee meetings, regulation of lobbyists, limitations on "earned income," public reports of wealth, health, and medical records, etc.

If corruption persists after all these methods of control are perfected, and there is good reason to believe that it will, the next step obviously would be to insure that potential officeholders were of such character as to be above and beyond corruption. A state run by the pure, the good, the incorruptible is an idea as old as Plato. The "guardians" of the state should be, he said, selected and given special training. They should be "watched from their youth upwards," tested by "toils and pains." They should be tried with "pleasures" also. Those who come "out of the trial victorious and pure" should be, according to Plato, appointed as guardians of the state.

In this process of selection, the FBI could play a crucial role. Beyond investigations of announced candidates, it could run scam tests of their integrity and publish results before the election date, or it could leak such results. Candidates could be graded as to the level of their integrity in the transition period, before the tests of purity and the Platonic training program were perfected. According to press reports, FBI Director Webster already has taken this role upon himself in calling Senator Pressler, who resisted the FBI bribe offers, to tell the Senator that "he had performed beautifully under pressure."

The *Washington Star* discounted the concern of some persons over the ABSCAM project, and dismissed criticism that ABSCAM employed the methods of dictatorship. "Who, for example, are the candidates for dictator?" asked the *Star*, evidently unaware that dictatorship is possible without a dictator.

It may be time for us to consider Brecht's suggestion, made to the Communist government of East Germany when that government expressed disappointment in the workers who rioted in June of 1953, that the "government dissolve the people and elect another."

More and More Things We All Could Be Protected From

A Federal Trade Commission judge recently ruled that the makers of Poli-Grip are guilty of misleading advertising. He came to this conclusion after observing a television commercial that featured persons using Poli-Grip or Super Poli-Grip. These products are described as adhesives for holding dentures (formerly known as false teeth) in place.

The faulted ad showed a male picnicker eating fried chicken "with gusto and confidence," according to the report, while a chorus sang, "Yeah, eat as you like. Take a good healthy bite of life." The camera then shifted to a female picnicker who was, according to the judge, "enthusiastically eating corn on the cob," while an announcer's voice said, "So what if you wear dentures."

The judge is obviously right. With or without dentures, and I assume with or without Poli-Grip adhesive, one cannot eat corn on the cob or fried chicken or spareribs with confidence. One cannot eat them without embarrassment and some discomfort. Politicians know this. They are the targets of photographers who try to catch them in the embarrassing position of biting into a leg of chicken, handling a greasy sparerib, or trying to get a piece of corn free from its position between teeth before rising to speak. A bit of corn, a shred of chicken, or a string of dry sparerib between the teeth does not make for easy speaking.

Judge Brown, the FTC judge, is, if anything, a thorough man. He did not give denture-wearers or the general public a superficial explanation of his ruling. He included the scientific information that the "very manner in which many dentures are constructed results in the situation where the front teeth are virtually useless for biting and only serve cosmetic purposes." For many denture-wearers, according to Judge Brown, only the back teeth serve a truly useful function when they "become the surface for pulverizing the food."

One might assume that denture-wearers, after one experience with corn or fried chicken while using Poli-Grip or Super Poli-Grip, might decide not to buy it again. Evidently, the FTC wishes to protect denture-wearers from the initial mistake of believing in Poli-Grip, thus saving them the expense of the purchase and also the false pleasure that might have come from anticipating the joy of once again eating corn on the cob, fried chicken, spareribs, and hard apples.

The judge, if his decision survives review by the FTC, will have saved denture-wearers from delusion, illusion, and—following either or both—the horror of disillusion. According to T. S. Eliot, disillusion is a dangerous state of mind: for, if one rests in it, it can become an illusion in itself. The prospect of masses of disillusioned denture-wearers is frightening to contemplate.

Meanwhile, the Food and Drug Administration, not to be outdone, has done what it says has never been done before. It has drafted a model ordinance to insure the cleanliness of the country's two hundred thousand grocery stores. If state and local jurisdictions follow the FDA proposal, food will have to be stored at least six inches off the floor. (This is not high enough to escape cockroaches, which have been found in great numbers on New York City buses.) Delicatessen beef will have to be cooked at an internal temperature of 130 degrees. Store employees will have to keep their fingernails trimmed and clean (length of fingernails not prescribed). Each employee will have to have his or her own towel (no more roller towels) and chopping blocks will have to be made of hard maple or a similar nonabsorbent wood.

Meanwhile, Wheaties has escaped a court action against Bruce Jenner commercials by proving that Jenner, an Olympic champion, really does eat them, as he says in the ad.

There is no end to the products from which we could be protected. In a casual examination of *Carte Blanche* magazine for November-December 1977, I found advertisements for an information machine, which promises automatic learning, for a "bunny sleeper," a kind of night garment that no female "will be able to resist," for the "best prime rib" in twenty-five different towns, and for a golf ball that is guaranteed to take three to five strokes off anybody's score.

As President Carter said, life is not fair.

Judging the Cabinet

In a parliamentary system, like that in England, voters usually know before an election who the principal members of the next cabinet will be. In the United States, voters can only speculate, with the help of columnists, who have not been very accurate in their predictions of who will be appointed by the newly elected Presidents. Occasionally, a candidate will hint at prospective appointments. In this year's campaign, only one likely candidate, Gerald Ford, named a possible appointee. Ford said that, if elected, he would make Henry Kissinger, Henry and God willing, his Secretary of State. This announcement was looked upon as a sign of weakness, as violating the cult of secrecy about future cabinet nominees.

Immediately after election, however, the timidity and hesitation that marked the candidate disappear. Presidents-elect begin to talk about the important choices they are prepared to make, and soon they begin to name prospective cabinet officers. It is as though election had given them the special grace of office, not unlike the gift of infallibility that follows from a papal election.

Ronald Reagan is expected to begin announcing his

cabinet choices this week. He has been getting outside advice, solicited and unsolicited, from columnists and political commentators. I would not presume to offer such advice. But in judging the selections Reagan does make, it will be useful to recall the qualifications, characters, and performances of cabinet members in past administrations.

I would rate George Marshall as the best Secretary of State in recent decades. Marshall was experienced in war and in peace; he was pragmatic. He saw foreign policy as an extension of national character and interests. He was a "historian." The worst Secretary of State was Dean Rusk, although pushed hard by John Foster Dulles. Dulles laid down the ideological lines for the cold war "confrontation," "massive retaliation," "the immorality of neutralism," and so on. He also arranged covenants, executive agreements, and treaties to sustain these moral judgments. Rusk, succeeding Dulles after a brief interlude, accepted the ideological dicta and took action to support them. He was to Dulles what Cromwell was to John Calvin.

The general conclusion is that the Secretary of State should not be an ideologue. The appointee should not be from a family with strong traditions in the religious ministry, nor be a geopolitical thinker, nor be schooled in the balance-of-power theory of the Austro-Hungarian empire. And, preferably, he or she should not have been "with" a foundation or, as they say, "of" an institution, like Brookings.

The best Secretary of the Treasury in the last fifty years probably was Henry Morgenthau of the Roosevelt administration. He was skilled in politics and in finance, informed of world affairs. Among recent Secretaries, three deserve praise: Henry Fowler, and his successor, Joseph Barr, of the Johnson administration, and George Shultz, of the Nixon administration. All three understood that the United States dollar was a force for stability and economic growth at home, and a force for order in world affairs. The worst recent Treasury Secretary was John Connally, who in a short term achieved a significant failure by cutting the dollar free, and letting it float—or, in a more appropriate Texas image, letting it loose on the world monetary range with no more than a hair brand to identify it.

The best Attorney General of modern times was Francis Biddle, who held that office under Roosevelt and under Truman, with William Rogers of the Eisenhower administration as a runner-up. Both Biddle and Rogers kept the office above politics. Both understood that the Attorney General was the top law officer in the land. Both probably would have resigned if it had been suggested to them that a special prosecutor be appointed to handle matters under their jurisdiction. The worst Attorney General of our times was John Mitchell, for politicizing the Justice Department even to the point of involving it in campaign politics. The Attorney General should not be the campaign manager of the President who appoints him. Preferably, this person should not be from the President's own political party. Nor, for that matter, from the President's family.

Cabinet positions other than the three above are of lesser order, or should be if properly conceived and administered. They are primarily service and executive offices, rather than policy-making ones.

Louis Johnson, Secretary of Defense under Truman, was the last Secretary to stand against the growth of the military-industrial complex. Melvin Laird, Secretary of Defense under Nixon, was a militarist, but he directed and controlled the expansion. Laird's political experience was a good preparation. His record supports the argument that the Secretary of Defense should be drawn from Congress.

The worst Secretary of Defense must be Robert McNamara. He brought to the office the arrogance of the automobile industry, which previously had been represented by Charlie Wilson of General Motors. One sure conclusion is that the Secretary of Defense should not be a former automobile executive. A football coach might do, or possibly two: one for defense and one for offense.

The Postmaster General is no longer a member of the cabinet. But without question, the best Postmaster General was James Farley of the Roosevelt administration. He ran the post office and also the Democratic party. He kept politics in the post office where it could do little harm. He recognized that politics is like pigeons. If it is concentrated in one building, or in one department, you should not scatter it to others.

The worst Postmaster General was Arthur E. Summerfield of the Eisenhower administration. He let politics get out of the post office, and let the service deteriorate. Then he took up pornography and censorship. *Lady Chatterley's Lover* was banned from the mails, as was Aristophane's *Lysistrata*. The ban on the second item was lifted when Summerfield learned that the play had been written over 2,000 years before he moved to ban it.

The best Secretary of Labor was Frances Perkins. The poorest was Martin Durkin of the Eisenhower administration. Durkin had been a union member. Perkins was a graduate of Mount Holyoke. The lesson is obvious.

The best Secretary of Agriculture was Charlie Brannan, who delighted in arguing with Agriculture Committee members. The worst was Ezra Taft Benson, a bishop of the Mormon Church. A good rule for picking a Secretary of Agriculture is to get someone from the opposite party to take the job, someone who will not introduce religion into the department, and someone who knows that ethnic jokes, which may be accepted quite without prejudice by farm audiences, are not generally acceptable. If hard-pressed, the President might look to Minnesota, which in recent years has become the mother of Secretaries of Agriculture.

Harold Ickes of the Roosevelt cabinet was a model Secretary of the Interior. He not only was a conservationist, but was also a capable defender of his policies, able to draw criticism away from the President, and unquestionably politically helpful. Ickes was credited with typing Thomas Dewey, Roosevelt's opponent in the 1944 Presidential election, as "the little man on the wedding cake." He once defended the government policy of killing young pigs to reduce the supply of pork during the Depression by saying that he had "never known a pig that died of old age." The worst Secretary of the Interior was Douglas McKay of the Eisenhower administration, appointed for no discernible reason other than that he had been Governor of Oregon, a state with many trees. Before becoming Secretary, he had owned and operated a Chevrolet dealership.

The best Secretary of Health, Education, and Welfare, now the Department of Health and Human Services, was Wilbur Cohen, a nonpolitical career person. Wilbur knew the programs and knew how to administer them. He never complained of the burdens of the office or suggested that they were beyond his powers. He left the proposing of new programs to the elected politicians. The worst HEW

Secretary possibly was John Gardner, who resigned from the office in protest over "priorities" and other things. Gardner was miscast; he misunderstood the office. Gardner would have been a good person to preach the Crusades or proclaim the westward movement in the United States, but he was not the person to put in charge of the march to Jerusalem or of a wagon train passing through Indian territory. The guiding rule in picking a Secretary of Health and Human Services is that his or her motto should be "Sufficient unto the day are the problems already assigned to this department." The Secretary should not reach out seeking more authority, as did Joseph Califano when he challenged the Secretary of Agriculture for jurisdiction over killing chickens.

Appointing a Secretary of Commerce is one official act in which no President should fail. The Secretary of Commerce should be a nice person, decent, contented, full of pleasantries, with no further political ambitions, ideally with no ambitions of any kind. He or she should be able to report encouraging or discouraging business reports with equal assurance and optimism. The best Secretary of Commerce in recent administrations was Luther Hodges, in the Kennedy administration. Luther wore a fresh flower in his coat lapel each day.

The new departments—Housing and Urban Development, Transportation, Energy, and Education—have not been in existence long enough to permit objective standards for Secretaries like the ones I have discussed. In any case, President-elect Reagan has said he would eliminate some of these.

Volunteer Army
Not Working

It's becoming popular to excuse bad judgments in politics by saying that the ideas at the root of the judgments were "bad ideas whose time had come." Thus, when the revenue-sharing program turned out to be highly unsatisfactory to state and local politicians, as well as to federal office-holders, one defense offered was that "revenue-sharing was a bad idea whose time had come." They say that the power and sweep of the general idea was so strong that it was impossible to make the necessary fine or subtle distinctions. They say that the cockle had to grow with the wheat.

Now, even many of those who used to say that the proposal for a volunteer army was a good idea whose time had come (both militarists and civil libertarians supported the idea) are having second and third thoughts.

As things have worked out, the military has been unable to attract enough personnel able to understand and operate complicated and highly technical military equipment. It has been unable to attract a cross section of the United States population in order to make the army reasonably representative of the nation itself.

Even though standards for admission have been lowered and additional benefits have been offered (such as $1,500 in cash bonuses or $2,000 in educational aid to young people who enlist for six years in the Army Reserve or the National Guard), neither the regular military forces nor the Reserve and National Guard have been able to attract enough persons to reach their goals. All four services—army, navy, air force, and marines—have missed their recruiting targets for the third quarter in a row.

Under pressure to deliver their quotas, recruiters have resorted to a variety of devices. A New York station put each recruit's name into the computer system three times, simply by varying the first name and initials; thus, John Edward Smith could also be entered as John E. Smith or as J. Edward Smith. The triplication did not show up until several months later. Other recruiting stations enlisted illegal aliens. Recruiting personnel in some stations coached enlistees for their entrance exams and even doctored records.

The Marine Corps, evidently following the policy of Mohammed, who, when he could not get the mountain to come to him, decided to go to the mountain, announced recently that it is reducing its numerical strength by about 10,000 persons. By the end of 1978, the Ready Reserve had declined from 1,600,000 persons to 360,000.

It is fortunate that the volunteer-army idea has not worked. For it was a screen for the creation of a mercenary army, which Alexis de Tocqueville and others warned is the most dangerous kind of military establishment in a democracy.

Obviously, registration for potential military service should be resumed. And selective drafting by lottery, according to the determined military needs of the country, should be introduced. Voluntary service in the Reserves or National Guard should be an alternative for those who wish not to take the risk of the lottery.

A continuing test for patriotism, through the acceptance of a draft lottery, is a test and a challenge to which I believe the young people of the country would respond. They should not be judged without trial.

A military establishment that reflects the culture of the nation is likely to be a much better base from which to make moral and political judgments about military action than an unrepresentative group moved to military service by economic need or social inadequacy.

Pigeons
Not in the Grass, Alas:
The Mess in Washington

The General Services Administration has announced that it is taking on once again the perennial problem of pigeons in Washington. Possibly, GSA is moved by an earnest desire to help the newly elected President carry out his campaign promise (one that is made by challenging Presidential candidates every Presidential election year) to clean up the mess in Washington. Or, possibly, GSA is making a last-ditch attempt to demonstrate that it is a useful agency, in order to escape the Reagan axe, despite its recent record of not being able to perform very satisfactorily its statutory responsiblities of keeping track of typewriters, desks, paper clips, and other office supplies.

GSA's announced program is not one of limited objectives. It does not contemplate the use of halfway measures. It will seek to achieve the total depigeonization of Washington, through extermination of what is known as "the Federal Triangle flock." Mere reduction of the number of pigeons in the flock will not satisfy, nor will confinement of the birds to specific areas or buildings.

Traditional devices for frightening pigeons, such as stuffed owls and mechnical snakes, will not be used.

Chemicals like Roost-No-More and Avitrol are not scheduled for use, since neither worked well in the past. Roost-No-More was introduced for the Nixon inauguration in 1973. A slimy substance, it was smeared on the trees along the parade route. The slime was supposed to cause the birds to skid off branches along the way, and, consequently, in discouragement or frustration, to fly away. But Roost-No-More was not satisfactory. The birds ate the chemical and many ended up, or down, sick or dead. The Washington Humane Society was disturbed.

The threat posed by pigeons to Presidential parades, it should be noted, is not as great as it was in earlier times, when the open convertible was used to transport elected Presidents and other notable persons down Pennsylvania Avenue. The popular style today is the turret-top limousine, in which the President, or another VIP, exposes only the upper parts of his body, with arms upstretched, looking, depending on his mood, like someone either sinking slowly in quicksand or arising from the grave in response to Gabriel's horn. In either case, the turret-top considerably reduces the target area for pigeons.

In the summer of 1979, another controlled attack on the pigeons was initiated. A company hired by the government drugged the pigeons using corn treated with Avitrol. Avitrol was meant to drive the pigeons off by giving them some kind of seizure. It turned out to be lethal, and public protest moved the government to abandon that effort.

Two years ago, the Carter administration launched an even more subtle attempt on the lives of pigeons in Washington, with the effort to re-establish the peregrine falcon in the skies above the nation's capital. This project was conducted by the Department of the Interior, which claimed that pigeon eradication was not its main purpose.

Pigeon deaths would be only a "natural fallout"; the primary purpose was the restoration of the falcon. Nature and ecology would be held responsible for the pigeon deaths. The Humane Society, the conservationists, the friends of endangered and deprived species, could have no cause to object. The Interior Department did succeed in hatching four young hawks atop one of the departmental buildings, and hopes ran high that the peregrines would, in accordance with the Scriptures, "increase and multiply." Alas, not so. The young hawks have flown. Of the four that hatched, one is reported to have been found dead in Baltimore after flying into a building, possibly standing where once a tall pine grew. Another died of sickness, or of gunshot, on Long Island. Two are not accounted for.

The GSA evidently has given up on sound as a means of discouraging pigeons, and will not expand a system now in place on the White House grounds. President Carter once invited to the White House a group of poets. These sensitive creatures, normally attuned to the sweet notes of the lark, the thrush, the cuckoo, and the mockingbird, were startled to discover the strident recorded sounds of the frightened starling coming from a wired magnolia tree as they waited in line to be received by President Carter.

The GSA spokesman does say that as a back-up measure, the agency may recondition and reactivate the long-abandoned electric-wiring systems placed on many government buildings decades ago in a vain attempt to discourage starlings and pigeons from roosting and nesting on the cornices of government. The core of the current GSA plan, however, is a no-nonsense approach. Basically, it entails spreading box traps on roofs throughout the Federal

Triangle, and then poisoning the captured birds with chemicals such as carbon monoxide and chloroform.

This project may give the GSA something to do until President Reagan moderates his current adamant stand against redecorated government offices, but is is doomed to failure. Pigeon experts know that pigeons cannot be exterminated. At most, they can be moved about. The greatest American practitioner of the science of moving pigeons about was one Lewis Neid, of St. Paul, Minnesota. The Neid technique might not work in Washington, but it was perfect for St. Paul. At the height of Neid's career, St. Paul had only three tall buildings: the state Capitol on a hill to the north, the archdiocesan cathedral on a hill to the northwest, and the First National Bank building on what was called the upper levee. Neid hired himself out as pigeon-remover to Church, State, and commerce, but never to all three simultaneously. In this way, the pigeons always had a safe haven in at least one of the three buildings, while each of the three great estates of St. Paul could feel that they were rid of pigeons most of the time. Possibly, a Neid-like program, challenging every pigeon sense, might drive the birds to Crystal City or to Rosslyn, where all buildings are nonhistoric, and will long remain so.

The Neid experience and theory is sustained by most scholarly and scientific judgment. Eric Simms, the noted British ornithologist, concludes in his book *The Public Life of the Street Pigeon*, published in 1979 and based on a study of the six-thousand-year history of pigeons:

Pigeons are dependent upon man, and as long as man is around, the pigeon will be too.

While man continues to live in decaying houses and retains

105

his wasteful and idle habits, there will be an attraction in our towns and cities for the pigeon. The only way to control the pigeon is to live in a clean and tidier way.

The street pigeon, Simms says, is not "an endangered species." He might have added: not by nature, or by man, or by the General Services Administration.

Aardvark and
the Right of Privacy

For centuries, the aardvark has led a quiet, retiring, semi-nocturnal life in South Africa. Even after it was moved from its native habitat into the zoos of the world, it shunned not only the public light, but also light itself. It is now an endangered species (actually an endangered genus, for the aardvark is both genus and species). But the aardvark is not in danger of physical extinction like the snail darter or the lousewort, or the various kinds of bandicoots; it is in danger of losing what it appears to value more than life itself, its privacy.

Ten years ago, I wrote a poem entitled "The Aardvark," hoping that anyone who read the poem would conclude that he or she knew as much about the aardvark as anyone would want to know, and lose interest in the animal. Among other things, the poem pointed out, aardvarks cannot look and listen at the same time; they cannot see red or green, or pink or purple, or Roman brown; they see only gray both night and day; they eat only termites, especially those that have eaten the dead wood of the tree of knowledge; with long tongues they speak a thin language no one can understand; and because aardvarks have no gizzards, they think only of soft food.

I could have added that, by one report of an observant naturalist, the aardvark will turn vegetarian, but only to eat wild cucumber that has grown from seeds germinated in the excrement of another aardvark. Moreover, aardvarks, according to students of evolution, did not evolve from anything, nor are they evolving into anything, like horses or kangaroos. The aardvark is a member of the Chordata phylum, which has in its early stage of growth a notochord, a rodlike flexible structure, instead of a backbone. But I thought no one would want to know any more about the aardvark.

A noted theologian long ago observed that the worst heresies are those that are closest to the truth. His point is well demonstrated in the common perception of the aardvark, for the aardvark is like many other animals, possibly like all other animals. It is like a pig in some respects, like a rabbit, like a donkey, like a badger, noticeably like an anteater. But no animal is like an aardvark, for if an animal is like an aardvark, it is an aardvark. In other words, the aardvark metaphor is not reversible. In the natural world, the aardvark is the ultimate metaphor, as in the supernatural order, it is accepted that God is like all his creatures. But it is wrong to say that some creature is like God. Lucifer, the angel who fell or was cast down from heaven, tried to reverse, to his or its sorrow, this metaphor.

A few months ago, an aardvark was brought onto the Johnny Carson show and displayed by a curator from the San Diego zoo. In March, the American Association of Aardvark Aficionados, not content to be as publicity-shy as the object of their interest, declared in a letter to the *New York Times* that the first week in March was National Aardvark Week. The association also announced that a Miss American Aardvark contest would be held at the Philadelphia zoo. This announcement indicated either ignorance or surprising knowledge on the part of the members of that society, since aardvarks, unlike pandas, for example, are sexually very modest and undemonstrative. It is, according to the curator from the San Diego zoo, very difficult to distinguish sexes among the aardvarks. In fact, there are some experts who say that even the aardvarks are somewhat confused on this point.

Animal Kingdom magazine could not remain silent. It reported the death of an aardvark called Bronx, who, after living quietly without progeny in the New York zoo for thirteen years, had been moved to a zoo in Miami, where in the ten years remaining before his death, he sired seventeen offspring, all born in captivity, the penultimate indignity for an aardvark.

At least one national columnist, presumably in need of material for a column, has taken up the aardvark and treated it, in the common manner of columnists, disrespectfully.

Most recently, Congressman John Anderson, running as an independent candidate for the Presidency, and insisting that he had no intention of establishing a political party, has announced that he is considering the aardvark as the totem animal for his movement. This would be the ultimate violation of the aardvark.

Jefferson's Declaration—
Good Politics,
Good Literature

G. K. Chesterton, the English essayist, once wrote, "America is the only nation in the world that is founded on a creed. That creed is set forth with dogmatic and even theological lucidity in the Declaration of Independence; perhaps the only piece of practical politics that is also theoretical politics and also great literature."

The creed to which he referred was expressed in these words: "We hold these truths to be self-evident, that all men are created equal, that they are endowed by their creator with certain unalienable rights, that among these are life, liberty and the pursuit of happiness."

The July 4, 1776, declaration followed by only a few weeks the Virginia Declaration of Rights (of June 12, 1776). The document, attributed to George Mason, asserted, "All men are by nature equally free and independent and have certain inherent rights." Mason listed these rights as "the enjoyment of life and liberty, with the means of acquiring and possessing property, and pursuing and obtaining happiness and safety."

There are no notes nor records on why the language of the Jefferson declaration differed from that of Mason.

Scholars have reflected and commented on the omission of any reference to property rights in the Jefferson text.

Conservative politicians and commentators have deplored the omission. And a few have held that if the drafters of the declaration had anticipated the income tax, they would have emphasized property rights.

Few persons have noted or commented on the much more interesting question of why the "pursuit of happiness" was included among the unalienable rights.

It is certain that the men who wrote and approved the Declaration of Independence were not careless draftsmen. They were men who, if their revolution failed, were likely to be hanged or shot as traitors, rather than suffering the limited disgrace of losing an election or the harsher treatment of exile to San Clemente.

The declaration was not merely an inspirational piece of propaganda. It was not the product of a task force or of a brain-storming session. It was not drafted after a crash course in the great books. It was intended to be what Chesterton saw it to be: the ideological text upon which a government and a nation would be founded.

Present in the thoughts of the men at the drafting was the wisdom of the past, the record of history. The inclusion of the "pursuit of happiness" as an unalienable right was not an accident. Nor was the word "happiness" included as a catchall, with a vague and undefined and overly comprehensive meaning such as is given to it today.

In 1776, the word was still used in the plural, as it had been used in 1601, for example, by Robert Johnson, who wrote that nature had heaped on England "those delightful happinesses." Thomas Otway, writing in 1678, said, "Ten thousand happinesses wait on you." Colley Cibber in

1739 wrote, "It was therefore one of our greatest happinesses." As late as 1885, Charles Haddon Spurgeon declared, "Heaped up happinesses [in the plural] belong to that man who fears the Lord."

The Declaration of Independence offered as a right only the "pursuit of happiness." This undoubtedly included the right to pursue property as a form of happiness, or as "a happiness."

John Adams, in two separate comments on the American Revolution, identified the different happinesses. One, which he saw as personal, was in the acceptance of the inconveniences of independence, in a changed and more austere way of life. The other was "public happiness," defined as a willingness on the part of the colonists to take public responsibility, to make common decisions and to follow those decisions—a spirit that he said was so strong among the colonists that the Revolution was bound to succeed.

The inclusion of the pursuit of happiness as an unalienable right was a unique act of genius on the part of those, principally Jefferson, who drafted the Declaration of Independence. It distinguishes that document from all other declarations of national or international political purposes.

The Sacking of
Sir Peter Ramsbotham

The sacking of Sir Peter Ramsbotham as British Ambassador to the United States is a serious matter in itself, but more so for the fact that it is being done so badly. The British have always been good on style, even when short on substance.

Sir Peter is being removed as Ambassador to the country that was the first of Her Majesty's colonies (then His Majesty's colonies) to break away from the Crown some two hundred years ago. He is being made Governor of Bermuda, the only remaining Crown colony of what was once the British empire. It is expected that Sir Peter will be there as Governor when the flag is run down. He deserved a better going-away.

Sir Peter served well as Ambassador to the United States. He did all of those things expected of a British Ambassador. He did them well, despite the fact that he labored under two handicaps with which previous British Ambassadors had not had to contend—a floating pound and a floating Queen's Birthday Garden Party.

The pound has been floating during the whole of Sir Peter's term in the United States. How different it was to be Ambassador when the pound was supported, sometimes heroically, as the one fixed point in the whole spectrum of unstable currencies. And how different it was even when the pound was devalued, as it was in November of 1967 and again in December of 1971. For whenever the pound was devalued, the Ambassador was expected to make a public statement—with stiff upper lip—and a judgment on the state of the world. (And, after all, devaluation was the only way in which the subject peoples and the nations served by the pound could be taxed.) But a floating pound allowed for no heroic statements, no marked days.

More serious than the bearing of the uncertain pound on the Ambassador's performance was the uncertainty that arose regarding the Queen's Birthday Garden Party. That garden party, normally held in the first or second week of June, was the absolute in Washington social and diplomatic life. To be invited to the party showed that one was politically and socially alive. Not to be invited was cause for self-examination, if not for despair. (I was dropped for some reason, as I recall, in 1968, restored to the list around 1971-72, and then dropped again. But by that time, the party was not what it had once been.)

In the old days, one could make excuses for being excluded from other embassy parties, even White House parties. One could say that the embassy was not important; that the Ambassador was new or the country was new; that the embassy or its grounds were too small; that one had turned down the last invitation. Almost any defense would do. But not so with the Queen's Birthday Garden Party. It was not small; about two thousand persons were invited. The grounds were large. There was continuity from one Ambassador to the next, even though the government of England had changed.

The week during which the invitations were known to be in the mails was one of uneasiness and anxiety in Washington. Socialites, diplomats, and politicians waited for the letter carriers. If no invitation came within the first two or three days, a call to the post office or a visit to the missent-mail department was the first resort of the anxious. By the sixth or seventh day, the desperate were driven to call the social secretary at the British embassy.

Others took their fate quietly, and hoped for the next June. They knew that for one year, they would have to wait in anticipation of again enjoying the pleasures of the garden party—of champagne, slightly warm; of strawberries, slightly fermented; of the cream, slightly sour. They would have to wait for the experience of seeing women appear, as you talked to them, to be growing shorter and tilting as their narrow heels sank into the soft turf of the garden, and then seeing them recover full height and balance as they subtly pulled their heels out of the turf to regain their footing or heeling.

During Sir Peter's term, fewer persons were invited to the party. The date became uncertain; the time of the day was changed. Worst of all, on occasion the guests were treated in separate classes.

Sir Peter served through all of this with dignity and distinction. But after enduring much, he is to have no quiet, honored leaving.

Sir Peter has been a fuddy-duddy, we are told, not approved by the new Foreign Secretary. All is to be changed. The new Ambassador will not be a fuddy-duddy; he is not a bird-watcher. He does, we are told, sometimes listen to classical music for twelve hours at a stretch, and sometimes plays bridge until four in the morning. And he has a house of glass and steel and Hessian walls. (Hessian material is called "gunny sack" by Americans, "chaff bag" by Australians, "burlap" by the sophisticated.)

The new Ambassador is to be the image or incarnation of what the British government conceives the Carter administration to be. He is also to be the image of the new England. In fact, he is to be a double image.

Surely, Robert Morley, who in his television ads projects the image of the old England, the England one should visit, will have to go. A new, sharp, younger Englishman will have to come on—urging us, with pictorial support, not to go to England to see the changing of the Guard at Buckingham Palace, but to see an English tank division on maneuvers. (After all, the British invented the tank—not the horse or the cavalry.) Not to see the cottages and manor houses, but a new high-rise or two and public housing in the steel towns. Not to see the Tower of London, but the newest, scientifically designed English prison. England has changed.

As one who first learned of England at his grandmother's knee, as she told of Cromwell's treatment of the Irish, the great hunger, and the eviction of the cottagers, I am moved by the threat of this new image of England to say:

> God save England
> God save the Queen
> God save Sir Peter Ramsbotham
> and also Robert Morley
> the Pound
> and the Queen's Birthday Garden Party.

Say It Ain't So, George!

Television is a harsh and cruel instrument. It allows no privacy. Danger lurks in every television advertisement.

Take the case of Oakland Raider George Blanda, the man of ultimate reality or, if not that, a perfect and unassailable illusion. Recall George, the incomparable, perennial if not quite eternal, place kicker. Year after year, answering the call under pressure for the field-goal attempt and the point after touchdown. George rising from the bench, putting on his helmet, and then—at a good round and solid trot—moving to the place of testing. The lineup, the signals called, the snap, the hold, the kick, and then the referee's arms raised to signal success. And then George, leaving the field, no leaps or jumps, no show of surprise or emotion, again at a steady trot. Then, as he neared the bench, the removal of the helmet, like a knight, after victory, a handshake from a teammate, a pat on the back, not more, and then repose on the bench, again waiting for the call.

The central act, the kick itself, was a thing of beauty and total coordination: the head, kept low, unafraid, the squared shoulders, the strong back and thighs, the hinged knee, the well-muscled calf, the firm ankle, and, finally, those bold and sturdy toes at the point of contact. Perfection.

And then the shock: the television ad with George, the second-most-trusted man in America, spraying his toes with a cure for athlete's foot. George with dermatophytosis? Old Fungus-foot? Not George! Perhaps lesser men, perhaps a baseball player like Mickey Mantle, but not George.

We knew that the fungus lived in locker rooms, in hotel bathrooms, even in Holiday Inns. The gymnasium of the House of Representatives has a foot bath at the entrance to the shower room. But there is in the Senate gym no foot bath of suspicion and, among the limited toiletries there supplied, no fungicide, but only shaving cream, shampoo, aftershave lotion, hair tonic, spray, and—on request —Grecian Formula.

Even the pharaohs had a problem. As the *Manchester Guardian* of July 1975 reported:

> Doctor Dean of Dublin determined:
> Lord Carnarvon did not die
> As newspapers reported in 1923
> Of a mosquito bite, that led to blood poisoning
> Which in turn led to pneumonia.
> Doctor Dean of Dublin determined:
> It was not the curse of Tutank-hamen
> That laid his Lordship low,
> Even though the lights in the Continental
>   Motel of Cairo
> Did dim, and go out at the moment of his death,
> And then come on Again.
>
> Doctor Dean of Dublin determined:

Say It Ain't So, George!

There was a fungus among the Pharaohs
That did in Lord Carnarvon,
Arthur Mace, and George Benedite, as well.

What was left but George Blanda and the United States Senate?

And now George's feet are gone. But there is more. Right there on television, in another commercial: George, looking a little apologetic, with an insecure smile, admitting something about his hair—that hair which we had all seen, slightly thinning, but still dark and ample, with a maturing gray around the edges and at the temples, when he doffed his helmet on the playing field, that hair just right in color, length, and composition, blowing a little in the wind, there in the late afternoon in slanted sun, or under lights at night; a consolation to men his age, a hope for younger men, a challenge to older ones.

And now the truth. George telling us: "No one really wants to be gray. I was getting too gray, but no phony dye job for me. Then a friend told me he used Grecian Formula. I didn't even know it. . . . The change was so gradual and looked so natural, no one even noticed. It left just a little gray. . . ."

Now we know it all, from head to toe. But hold, a further doubt. One more question to be answered: Is George on Geritol?

Say it ain't so, George. And if it is, don't tell us in a TV ad.

American History
and the NFL

What is the role of the National Football League in American history? This is the question a sportswriter asked of nine leading American historians and social and cultural commentators. I was reminded of this inquiry on reading in the paper that Roger Staubach, former quarterback for the Dallas Cowboys football team, was a prospective Republican candidate for the United States Senate in the 1982 election.

Of the nine experts who responded to the sportswriter's inquiry, only one found any positive social or cultural good coming out of the NFL. The views of the other eight ranged from those who said that they had no idea as to the NFL's influence on history, and no interest in trying to find out, to the absolute judgment of the historian Henry Steele Commager, who said the NFL has "no importance whatsoever."

The judgment of these scholarly experts was obviously bad. Perhaps they were too farsighted to see the effects of contemporary historical and cultural forces, or their insights were too penetrating to note surface changes. The fact is that the NFL has made a significant contribution in many cultural areas.

Roger, if he runs for the Senate, will join a number of other veterans of the league who have been candidates for Congress, including Congressman Jack Kemp, also a former quarterback, who was considered a possible running mate for Ronald Reagan in this year's Presidential campaign.

Major league baseball was represented for a few terms in the House of Representatives by Vinegar-bend Mizell, a relief pitcher. And the National Basketball Association now has Bill Bradley in the U.S. Senate representing New Jersey.

Several NFL stars or former stars have joined the entourages of Presidential candidates and have endorsed candidates.

The NFL has enriched the language of politics. It was a source of metaphors with which former Secretary of Defense Melvin Laird described aspects of the war in Vietnam. Bombing North Vietnam became known as "Operation Linebacker" and the failure of Vietnamese troops after U.S. withdrawal was explained as the failure of an "expansion team."

It has been suggested that our military establishment be organized as is the coaching of football teams, into a Department of Offense, to go along with the current Department of Defense.

In addition to these contributions to politics and to government, the NFL has contributed to the general patriotism of the country.

Singing of the national anthem, traditionally a part of the ritual of organized baseball, is now a part of the pregame ceremonies of the NFL. Patriotic display at baseball games is limited to singing the national anthem and flying the United States flag. Not so with football. Pregame trooping of the colors is customary and military-drill-team performances are commonly a part of the half-time program. A high point in demonstration of patriotic loyalty was reached in 1969, when at a game in Washington, thousands of flags were distributed to be waved, on direction, later during the game.

The NFL also has served to advance the cause of religion more openly and consistently than has baseball, for example. Players often in interviews give personal religious testimony. Pregame ceremonies in some cities include public prayer. A number of teams have regular chaplains, ranging from fundamentalist preachers to Catholic priests. No team carries a rabbi. In organized baseball, religion and prayer are largely a private and personal rather than a public act.

National Football League players have made notable contributions in other social and cultural areas, sometimes revealing things about themselves that they might, selfishly, keep secret. George Blanda's name on an advertisement for a treatment of athlete's foot somewhat disillusions those who thought he was kicking field goals with tired old feet, but not with fungus between his toes. Joe Namath asks people, in the "pursuit of happiness," to accept his recommendations for popcorn and panty-hose. Many players have joined in the drive to improve the American diet by changing from heavy to "lite" beer.

All these and other good things are flowing from the NFL, and it is only sixty years old.

Bring Back Polo: How to Kill October

The Federal Election Campaign Act of 1974, as amended after the Supreme Court found it defective on at least two major constitutional points, has properly been characterized as an incumbent insurance law. It is an insurance policy for the incumbent parties (the Democrats and Republicans and for House members and Senators in office at the time the bill was passed.

The election is also a rich man's license to hunt in the field of politics. It limits campaign contributions generally to $1,000 per contributor, per candidate, per campaign; but it allows a wealthy candidate running for Congress to spend his own and his family's money without limit.

In 1976, within the rules of this law, Representative H. John Heinz III (R,Pa.) spent over $2 million in his successful campaign to be elected to the Senate from Pennsylvania. His opponent, Representative William Green (D,Pa.), a man of limited means, could accept no personal contributions in excess of $2,000 ($1,000 for the primary and $1,000 for the general election).

Mr. Heinz was not the only candidate in 1976 to benefit from the special advantages given to the wealthy by the law. Spending from $200,000 to $400,000 of their own funds to run for House seats were Democrats Merlin Kerlock of Illinois, Cecil Heftel of Hawaii, Morgan Maxfield of Missouri, and Nick Joe Rahall of West Virginia.

The law, and its advantages, will not start a rush of the rich into politics. That movement has already gone far. But the law makes it easier for the rich to run, and makes them more secure in office once elected. As long ago as 1960, six out of the first seven Democratic members of the Senate Finance Committee were millionaires. Paul Douglas was the lone exception. Those Democrats represented relatively new wealth (oil and insurance) and were first- or second-generation rich. We made no estimate of the number of millionaires among the Republican members. But those whom we identified generally held wealth of more depth and seasoning—from mining, land, salt, and milling.

The reality is that state legislatures, governors' mansions, and the Congress of the United States are filling up with the rich, the sons of the rich, and an occasional daughter and widow. The interest of the new rich in politics is understandable. It is a natural aspect of their upward-mobility movement.

A du Pont is now governor of Delaware. A Rockefeller is governor of West Virginia. Both Arkansas and New York have had Rockefellers as governors in recent times. The Congress has had, or still does have, a Heinz of the 57 varieties, a Danforth of Purina, a Seiberling of tires, two Mortons of milling and salt, a Stuckey of candy, a Brock of candy, an Ottinger of plywood, a Reid of real estate and publishing, and so forth. In addition, there are and have been fathers and sons, brothers, mother and son, of old political names—such as Kennedys, Tafts, Boltons, Longs, and Goldwaters.

In the case of the established rich, the explanation of their movement to politics is more subtle and complicated. The reasons are to be found in deep cultural and psychological considerations. The rich today do not have security of place and of distinctive function in the social hierarchy. More particularly, they do not have such security in the world of sports and in the military.

Basketball, football, and hockey are clearly of and for the masses. Baseball, while somewhat exclusive, rests its exclusiveness on talent rather than on wealth or noble birth. Tennis, which once bore the mark of social superiority, has been popularized and vulgarized. Grass courts are all but gone. The game is now played on artificial turf, on wood, on clay, on plastic, and even on cement. Tennis white has been sacrificed to common taste and mixed colors. Rackets are made not only of wood, but also of steel, aluminum, and plastic. They are no longer strung with classical catgut, but with synthetic strings. The size of the racket is no longer standardized, on the technical justification that size was never defined by rules or by law. Tradition, which formerly controlled, is no longer sufficient. The rule of law is taking over. Whenever that happens, the role of the nobility is threatened.

In a comparable way, the democratization of the military has contributed to the social and psychological instability and insecurity of the aristocrats. Traditionally, even in the nineteenth century, there was in wartime a direct transition of persons from civil status to military status. The nobility, the wellborn, the gentry, became officers in the armies and in the navies. The peasants (later the farmers), the craftsmen (later the workers), the shopkeepers (later the clerks), became soldiers and seamen of the lower orders. Once the wars were over, the survivors returned to their previous positions and status in civilian society. Mass armies, modern warfare, and mechanization (which displaced the cavalry) changed all.

To restore order in both civil and military affairs two things are necessary: First, polo must be made, again, the exclusive game of the rich and of the wellborn. This should not be so difficult since although the game has declined, it has not been vulgarized. Second, the cavalry must be brought back as the branch of the military reserved principally for the noble and the wellborn.

Action on the cavalry is secondary. The key is polo.

The early history of polo is unclear, both as to how the game was played and when it was invented. But there is no uncertainty about the fact that it was a game played only by kings and princes, and by those in the higher order of the nobility, including horsed warriors, who in the beginning of mounted warfare were drawn from the upper classes.

When polo was brought to England from India in 1876, and then to the United States a few years later, it was a game exclusively for the better classes. Polo playing fields were located in the areas in which the rich lived: Evanston, Illinois; Old Westbury and East Aurora, New York; Westport, Connecticut; Grosse Pointe, Michigan; Delray Beach, Florida; Harbor Hills, Ohio; Santa Barbara, California. Later, they were in areas near old cavalry sites or communities of the new rich like Phoenix, Arizona, and Austin, Texas. The list of players with handicaps, as late as 1949, was made up almost exclusively of Anglo-Saxon names like Abbot, Campbell, Evans, Pedley, and Guest. There was an occasional McCarthy, one Milton Untermeyer, a Darryl Zanuck, and a William Ylvisaker.

The decline of polo resulted from many forces. It never

fully recovered from the Depression, and it was set back when the cavalry was abandoned in World War II. The automobile culture also had an adverse effect on polo. The new rich moved in on the game. Things fell apart.

The time has come to bring back the game, in pure and defined form. It must be restricted to the rich and to the wellborn. It must have a schedule that respects the seasons. It must be played only in the late summer and the fall. This time bridging two seasons has become a time of restlessness and discontent for the young rich, especially the males. There are things to be done in the winter: skiing, for example, and cruising in southern waters. Spring follows with golf, outdoor tennis, and early fly fishing. In the summer, there is the challenge of keeping cool, of Maine, of climbing mountains, of sailing in northern waters.

But what of the fall? "How do you kill October?" one rich young man was recently heard to ask sadly of another. With nothing challenging to do in the fall, and with politics the only thing going, the young rich have in greater and greater numbers been running for office. Even the old rich, beyond their polo-playing days (men like Averell Harriman), have dismounted and run for office.

The answer is polo. The restoration of the game would take care of the general need of the rich for action in the fall. It would also keep them out of politics.

The Columnist's Power
of Rash Judgment

All civilizations, even the most primitive ones, develop institutionalized and socially accepted persons or professions whose function it is to make rash judgments for the whole community.

In some societies, the function is performed by the witch doctor and the medicine man. In others, more advanced, the auspices and the augurs and the oracles take over. Some societies use prophets.

In our age and time and civilization, it is the columnist who is allowed—even expected—to make the ultimate rash judgment. Some columnists, on schedule, make as many as five rash judgments a week. Others make three. Some make them at random—not on schedule but when moved by the spirit. Some pronounce only once a week.

Since I have become a columnist, of the once-a-week variety, I have reflected seriously on the source of the special powers and privileges of the columnists.

Undoubtedly, columnists who develop within the newspaper world participate in the power traditionally claimed by editors. Just how this power originated and how it is passed on, even from editor to editor, is not clear—to say nothing of how it is passed from editor to columnist.

Papal power is carefully guarded and is passed on only after thorough study, prayer, and meditation by the College of Cardinals. There is a direct line, it is asserted, from the Apostle Peter to Paul VI, although the line is thin and wavering at a few points along the historical route.

Royal power traditionally descends through bloodlines. In some cases, the authority runs only on the paternal side, as it now does in Iran. In others, it can be passed on the maternal side and through the female line, as in England and Holland. Cousins occasionally have been cut in, and even illegitimate children, depending on circumstances and character and national need.

The origin and transfer of editorial power are much less clear than those of papal and royal powers. The beginning of editorial power is veiled in mystery of the past, although one historical school holds that it began when Moses descended from the mists of Mount Sinai and presented the first unsigned editorial.

The transfer of editorial power often takes place without biological or historical support. It is true that in some cases, editorial power is passed from father to son; in some cases, from father to daughter, or (skipping the intermediary generation) to grandson or granddaughter. Occasionally, it is given to a nephew or niece. Sometimes, it is exercised by the wife of a deceased editor, and she in turn may pass on the power. In some cases, the power is sold. This is somewhat like the sale of royal titles or the sale of church preferment, a practice called simony and generally condemned as a religious abuse.

In some cases, the power is passed by a kind of ordination, in which those who hold editorial power choose another and give the power to him or to her. The pope speaks "ex cathedra"—that is, from the official seat or chair of power. Editors speak from the editor's chair, and transfer power to others who may then, in similar manner, speak "from the seat of their pants."

Columnists are not quite of the class of editors, but they share some of the same power. Sometimes, they receive their power through natural or personal transfer, as when an editor becomes a columnist and signs his name. In other cases, reporters who have demonstrated editorial skills or proclivities are made columnists by sitting editors. Potential columnists, I have noted, cast their shadows before them as reporters, usually becoming more and more subjective in their reporting, and sometimes a little less accurate. They often add tag lines to their reports, such as "There is more to this story than has yet met the eye," or "What this means historically is uncertain," or, as one wrote the other day, "The clock of history is running."

My source of license and power as a columnist is not any of those claimed by editors or columnists who have come to their role through the newspaper profession. It arises from my service in the Senate of the United States. Other Senators have tested the strength of that power as columnists: Senator Goldwater, both in office and out, and Senator Humphrey, for a short time when he was out of office.

The Senate power is derived from the Constitution, which directs and empowers Senators to give advice (with or without consent) to the President. Sometimes, the need for that advice is so imperative that rashness is permitted.

The power is not lost when one leaves the Senate. Once given, it carries with the person, even to the point of sustaining him as a columnist.

Some Thoughts
on Having Given Scandal

In writing this column, I am breaking one rule that I have set for myself as a once-a-week columnist: not to read what other columnists have written; or, if for some reason I succumb to the temptation to read, or do so by accident, not to comment on what they have written.

This is a rule that I think once-a-week columnists should adhere to. Columnists who write five or even three columns a week should not be bound by any limits as to subject matter. They should be free to write about other columnists and columns, about their own children, if they have children, about nieces and nephews or grandchildren, about current events or past history. They should be free to include book reports, findings of private polls taken in places like Wausau, Peoria, and Fort Dodge, accounts of their own appendicitis operations, with or without acupuncture, and so forth.

I break my rule only because it appears that I have given scandal. Giving scandal is a most serious matter. According to the Scripture, it is better to have a millstone tied about one's neck and to be drowned in the depths of the sea than to scandalize the innocent. In this case, the scandal was not given to an innocent one, but to one we might expect to be immune to scandal, another columnist, Mary McGrory.

The scandalous act as reported was that of my embracing Henry Kissinger in public. Actually, as a careful observer would have noted, I did not embrace Henry. He embraced me. I was approaching him, expecting to shake hands with him, when quite suddenly he charged forward, getting his arms under mine. My response was at most a defensive counterembrace. This was the first and only time that I have been embraced by Henry Kissinger, whether in public or in private, although over the years, he and I have shaken hands several times. And we have twice had lunch together, once in public and once in private.

Mary evidently was so shocked that she sought solace in the words of James Rowe, the elder, to the end that I "would do anything." Now James Rowe has been around a long time. I would not say that he "would do anything"; but he has done some things, such as working hard in 1968 to get Democratic convention delegates who would support the pro-Vietnam-war position.

The fact is that I have a reputation of not being very demonstrative, of not being easily or visibly moved. I have been criticized for being aloof and unemotional, unresponsive, and even lacking in active compassion. (I have never been able to find out what the difference is between standard compassion and active compassion.) Against this background, the observed embrace might have been interpreted as showing a change of spirit on my part, as evidence that I had become a person of open emotion, responsive and forgiving.

But, no, the embrace apparently was cause for distress. Since in these times, by Presidential edict, one must avoid scandal and even the appearance of scandal, I have taken steps to prevent another Kissinger embrace.

I have talked with Henry! He is sorry and promises to be more careful in the future. His defense is that in his diplomatic travels, he became a somewhat indiscriminate embracer. In recent years, he embraced Egyptians and Israelis, Communists of various kinds, military dictators (if not Fascists), Chinese and Russians, leaders of states that are friendly to the United States and of states that are not considered to be our friends.

I admonished Henry that the standards for diplomats are different from those accepted by domestic politicans, and that what goes overseas does not necessarily go at home. Embracing by politicans stops at the water's edge, on the way home. What may be big in Beirut or Cairo or Peking or even Hanoi does not wash at the Washington Hilton.

Henry was abashed and apologetic and grateful, finally, for my admonition. He and I agreed that there will be no more embracing, and that for a time, until the scandal blows over, we will not even be seen together in public.

A Strange Inquiry

Mr. Harry M. Rosenfeld
Assistant Managing Editor
The Washington Post
1150 Fifteenth Street, N.W.
Washington, D.C. 20071

Dear Harry:

I have received your letter, including the questionnaire about Korean influence on the Senate. According to your letter, the questionnaire is similar to one that was sent to all members, and some former members, of the House of Representatives.

I do not understand why I was questioned as a former member of the Senate, but not as a former member of the House. Your letter did not explain. Was I chosen by lot? Did the *Post* think that I had some special connection or interest in Korea? Did the *Post* expect that I would respond to a request to inform on other members of Congress?

Having ruled out chance selection, I have looked to the questionnaire to find reasons for my inclusion in the list of possible respondees.

A Strange Inquiry

Your first question is whether I or any members of my Senate staff visited the Republic of Korea while I was in the Senate. Neither I nor any member of my staff, before or after January 1, 1970, officially visited the Republic of Korea. But I may have had a staff member along the way who fought in the Korean war.

The most prominent American politician to visit Korea was, I recall, Dwight Eisenhower. In his 1952 campaign, Eisenhower said that if elected, he would go to Korea. He did and, early in his administration, the division of Korea was agreed to. Following that agreement, arms and rice became principal shipments to Korea.

Which brings me to the second question, touching upon possible business associations with Korea. The *Post* might have suspected that I or my state has an interest in trade with Korea. We are not a great arms-producing state, though we are into rice. But here again, there is no Korean connection. Minnesota produces significant quantities of wild rice, but very little for export. The rice production and distribution is controlled by the Chippewa Indians. Insofar as I know, no Minnesota wild rice has been brokered through Tong Sun Park.

We do have one Oriental food interest, or at least we did have one. That was the operation of the Chun King Corporation, a company founded by an inscrutable Occidental from northern Minnesota, Jeno Palucci. Chun King is now owned by the parent company of R. J. Reynolds Tobacco.

As to the third question, about social connections with Koreans, my answer is wholly negative. Perhaps, though, I should state for the record that I have eaten *kimchi*—a fermented mixture of cabbage, onions, and fish, seasoned with garlic, horse-radish, red pepper, and ginger. (You may remember that this became an issue in the Vietnam war, when our Korean allies announced that without *kimchi* in their mess kits, they would not fight.) My *kimchi* experience occurred in a Korean restaurant formerly located in the Windsor Park Hotel. The restaurant was forced to move to northern Virginia when, following the admission of Mainland China to the United Nations, that country bought the Windsor Park Hotel for its Washington mission. Now I have to go over to Arlington for *kimchi*. The implications of diplomacy are far-reaching.

On first reading your third question, I was moved to respond to the name of Suzi Thomson. But, on reflection, I satisfied myself that I was confusing her with another person—one Sadie Thompson—to whom I was introduced many years ago by Somerset Maugham in "Rain."

Your fourth question is whether other foreign governments or their citizens are doing, or have done in the past, "about the same things the Koreans have." My answer is no. But it would not surprise me if some countries, such as Chile and Italy, might be of a mind to return the good services rendered in their politics by American agents. Perhaps we could work out a reciprocal campaign-interference agreement?

Your last question is whether I know of the involvement of other members of Congress. The answer is that I do not; but that if I did, I would not report it to the *Washington Post*.

The Press:
Self-examination,
Analysis, and Forgiveness

Thomas Babington Macaulay, nineteenth-century English statesman, historian, and essayist, observed that there was nothing so ridiculous as the English people engaged in one of their periodic bouts of self-criticism, remorse, and moral reform. Macaulay had never seen the American press, or elements of it, engaged in a similar act of apology, or defense, with accompanying promises of reform and purification.

Within recent weeks, two major papers have been purging themselves in public. The *New York Daily News* has accepted the resignation of a reporter after publishing a story about a British soldier in Northern Ireland. The soldier could not be found. Although the reporter insists that the soldier is real, he does not, it seems, have the name given to him in the report. The *News* did its thing quickly and relatively quietly.

Not so with the *Washington Post*, and the case of "Jimmy," the eight-year-old heroin addict, the creation of *Post* reporter Janet Cooke. Possibly, the *Post* could have satisfied itself, its readers, and critics with a quick apology had the Cooke story not received a Pulitzer Prize. The

Post response might also have been more restrained had not the *New York Times* been quick to editorialize on the case, declaring that "when a reputable newspaper lies, it poisons the community. Every other newspaper story becomes suspect."

This was laying it on a little heavily, and presupposes a degree of trust in the press somewhat beyond the reality. Unfortunately for the *Times*, at least one writer remembered that the *Times* itself had run, in 1964, a series of stories about a youth gang called Blood Brothers. The gang was never found, although it did have characteristics of other known gangs.

The *Post*, not surprisingly, and I think correctly, in its response to the "Jimmy" case, did not see it as having the far-reaching consequences noted by the *Times*. The *Post* saw the matter largely as a failure of character on the part of the reporter, Janet Cooke, and described the whole thing as a "scam," a "hoax," in which the *Post* was as much a victim, if not more of a victim, than the community and the "every other newspaper" referred to by the *New York Times*.

It is interesting to contrast the *Post*'s defense, in this case, with that offered by Richard Nixon in Watergate. President Nixon said that he was "responsible" for Watergate but not to blame. The blame he placed on all of us. The *Post* said that it was to be blamed but it was not responsible.

These two defenses mark an interesting switch. As a rule, politicians caught in difficulty, as has been the case of those picked up in the recent FBI scam, plead guilt but not responsibility. President Nixon, no ordinary politician, did the opposite. Nonpoliticians, corporate officials, or organizations, unlike the *Post*, usually plead responsibility but not guilt. The *Post*, no ordinary newspaper, did the opposite. The basic assumption seems to be that if the accused is not both responsible and guilty, all is forgiven.

A defense of the "Jimmy" story can be made, not absolutely but relatively; not the personalized one that some defenders of Ms. Cooke have been offering, with psychological overtones or undertones—she was under great pressure, having been picked for stardom at the *Post*; she was working in what one *Post* editor described as "our Watergate mode"—but an institutional or philosophical one.

There are distinctions among reporters and differences in how subject matter is reported. The works and methodologies of investigative reporters are distinguished from those of straight, or noninvestigative, reporters. Some reporters, particularly those who double as columnists, or anticipate becoming columnists, are prone to interpret the story as it is reported. Ms. Cooke wrote a story that sustained her judgment of conception of a situation. In other words, she fit the story to her conception, rather than affixing a conception to a story.

A reader of the news or a watcher of television is expected to distinguish between simple reports and in-depth reports. Television offers news, documentaries, and a new entry called the "docu-drama." An NBC presentation of selected and rearranged parts of the Jean Harris trial is an example, as is a program on the Iran hostages projected by CBS to be developed under the guidance and direction of Hamilton Jordan and Gerald Rafshoon, formerly of the Carter administration.

In broader context, beyond the limits of press principles, the "Jimmy" story falls easily within the bounds of one of the acceptable lies as classified by the poet Carl Sandburg, the lie told because people "can't help making a story better than it was the way it happened."

The press will survive this self-examination. It is not

likely to be worse off for the exercise; not like the Biblical character who, having driven out one evil spirit, was possessed by five others, so his last state became worse than his first; but more like what happens when monkeys at the zoo examine each other or themselves.

The work is serious. There is a great deal of scratching and scrutiny. Something is found, and usually eaten, after careful consideration. The monkeys appear to be deeply satisfied. Life at the zoo goes on much as it was before the examination.

Abe Lincoln: A Politician and Also a Poet

There is a long-standing tradition in America of scoffing at poets, especially if they show any interest in politics.

Few of the scoffers are familiar with the statement of Lytton Strachey: "It is almost always disastrous not to be a poet." Or with the words of Georges Clemenceau, great French political leader of the early twentieth century, who said that whereas poets and philosophers should not control government, politicians and political leaders who ignore what the philosophers and poets say do so at great peril.

Nor do the scoffers seem to know that Abraham Lincoln, considered by many to be the greatest American President, was a poet.

Lincoln was not a great poet. He did not need to be one in order to make his reputation as a writer. His prose was sufficient for that.

Lincoln wrote at least three poems of some length, seriousness, and quality—one of forty lines, one of sixty, and a third of eighty-eight lines. He was very strict and precise in the form within which he wrote. Each poem is divided into stanzas of four lines, the first and third line of each stanza having eight syllables, the second and fourth having six. The last syllable of the first line of each stanza rhymes with the last syllable of the third, and the last syllable of the second line with the last syllable of the fourth.

Lincoln's first known poem was written about 1845 and is called "My Childhood Home I See Again." With modesty, in a letter to a friend, Lincoln explains how he had come to write the poem: "In the fall of 1844, thinking I might aid some to carry the State of Indiana for Mr. Clay, I went into the neighborhood in that State in which I was raised, where my mother and only sister were buried, and from which I had been absent about fifteen years. That part of the country is within itself as unpoetical as any spot on earth: but still, seeing it and its objects and inhabitants aroused feelings in me which were certainly poetry; though whether my expression of those feelings is poetry is quite another question." This stanza is typical:

> I hear the loved survivors tell
> How nought from death could save
> Till every sound appears a knell
> And every spot a grave.

Lincoln's second poem is called "The Maniac." It was written about a young man named Matthew Gentry, who at the age of nineteen became insane. The poem describes the madness and then goes on to reflect on the why of it, and on the mystery of the mad boy's continuing to live while other persons, not mad but gifted, were taken by death.

The third Lincoln poem that has survived is on a lighter theme; it is called "The Bear Hunt." In the poem, he first describes the frontier:

Abe Lincoln: A Politician and Also a Poet

When first my father settled here,
'Twas then the frontier line:
The panther's scream, filled night with fear
And bears preyed on the swine.

Then he describes the hunt and, finally, after the bear is caught and killed, the argument over which hunter is to get the skin. While the argument is going on, one hound that had little to do with the catch arrives and

With grinning teeth, and up-turned hair
Brim full of spunk and wrath,
He growls and seizes on dead bear,
And shakes for life and death.

Lincoln ends the poem with a stanza of commentary, perhaps with political implications:

Conceited whelp! We laugh at thee
Nor mind, that not a few
Of Pompous, two-legged dogs there be
Conceited quite as you.

When Lincoln's friend A. Johnston (not the future Vice-President) suggested that he try to publish the poems, Lincoln agreed, but on condition that his name not be used. "I have not sufficient hope of the verses attracting any favorable notice to tempt me to risk being ridiculed for having written them," he wrote.

Lincoln's interest in poetry is shown in an earlier letter he wrote to the same Johnston, who had mistakenly attributed authorship of some other writer's poem to Lincoln. "Beyond all question, I am not the author. I would give all I am worth, and go in debt, to be able to write so fine a piece as I think that is," wrote Lincoln, the politician-poet.

On the Road

No other country in the world winnows out its would-be Presidents the way we do in the United States. There is a little of the Roman arena about it, a serious, grueling matter that also aims to provide a full measure of entertainment for the spectators.

Every four years, as sure as ritual, aspirants for the Presidency willingly submit themselves to the campaign trail, accepting its bumpiness, its humiliations, its diet, and its disappointments. The way is long, yet candidates spring up by the dozens. My heart goes out to them, for in the wise words of television correspondent Herb Kaplow, "No two campaigns are different." I know, and I remember it well.

It is not the stuff of history that grinds a candidate down. It is not the search for a broad and winning campaign strategy. It is not the unfounded attacks on your position, the cream pies with your name on them. Those one can handle, like the heat in the kitchen.

The abrasive part of any campaign is made up of small things—people and events that seem to count for little. But as the old hillbilly song has it: "It's the little things you do that count. Little things, my dear, but how they mount."

Take drivers, for example. Campaign chairmen and press secretaries are important, of course, but the humbling truth is that they are expendable and easily replaced. Not so with drivers. A reliable, steady automobile driver is integral to a comfortable and terror-free campaign, and every candidate should carry such a person with him from state to state. It is a question of self-defense, for if a candidate arrives driverless in a new city, he will be given over, like a prisoner to the Inquisitor, to the local drivers. These are picked for fidelity and service to the party and not for skill behind the wheel. The worst of all—the driver who haunts my campaign nightmares— is the kind with a pulse in his foot. He has a personal interior metronome that causes him to speed up and slow down for no reason apparent to others. The statesman in the back seat, intent on scribbling immortal rhetoric on the back of an evelope, has every chance of arriving at the next event whey-faced with nausea. There are, of course, no heroics to be demonstrated or votes to be gotten from an announcement that the candidate is carsick.

Much has been written about the Secret Service and the personal security it provides. This is a real and welcome umbrella, no mistake about it. Yet, the usefulness of these quiet, somber men does not stop there. They are excellent advance men and a valuable source of excuses for not going where one doesn't want to go anyway. Further, they are usually fine drivers. In three campaigns during which I had Secret Service escorts, I found only one with the dread pulse in his foot. The director of the unit burdened with me promised that this agent would be watched carefully.

There are dangers on the campaign trail against which the Secret Service can do little. These are the dangers that the candidate, out of zeal to be a good sport, inflicts upon himself. There comes a time in any campaign when softball is in season, and it is a must for candidates. I regard softball as the ultimate perversion of baseball—especially slow-pitch, Jimmy and Billy Carter's favorite, which I think is far more dangerous than hardball. (This is certainly true if one counts sprained ankles and thumbs.) Yet, if I may say so (in a magazine devoted to compelling photography), it is the importunities of photographers—who always want something visually arresting—that put the candidate in harm's way on the softball diamond.

The same goes for skiing, as George Romney found in New Hampshire. I learned only after making the commitment to play in an old-timers' hockey game in New Hampshire that "old-timers" was a term deceptively defined. Players merely had to be too old for the juvenile league and could not have played for the Boston Bruins. That left an appalling amount of room for talented players. I felt blessed to survive three turns on the ice and get my picture in *Time* magazine. My breathing returned to normal about two o'clock the next morning. Despite the risk, I could discern no difference in the outcome of the New Hampshire primary.

Another rule for thinking candidates is to stay away from horses. Even well-known horses are not to be trusted, especially in Fourth of July parades. A candidate on a sidling, skittish horse gives the voters second thoughts about the hand holding reigns of power. Unknown horses are not to be trusted under any circumstances.

A resolute candidate who is willing to risk being labeled a bad sport can avoid participant sports and their attendant risks. However, one must eat, and the dangers imposed on candidates by that fact may be the most fearsome of all. After all, President Harding died of food poisoning, or so they say. In the name of hospitality, candidates are threatened by good food and bad food, by food offered early in the day or late, by too much food and by too little food. It has sometimes seemed to me that the hot dish, usually a variation on macaroni and ground meat or, on Fridays, tuna fish and noodles, has become the sacramental offering—not to mention the burnt offering—of political campaigns. And then there are "ethnic" foods, which must be solemnly ingested to show solidarity with this or that group. Ethnic foods pose a much more powerful threat to candidates than do ethnic issues.

One must also sleep. When Walter Mondale announced that he was giving up his Presidential campaign in 1974 (a year in which one could not, in fact, run for the Presidency), he gave as one of his reasons his experiences in sleeping in motels.

Sleeping in motels can be an adventure, but it is scarcely traumatic enough to warrant dropping out of a campaign. The question for the candidate is what kind of bed arrangement he will find in his room: one double bed, two single beds, one double and one single, or two doubles. Alone in rooms with multiple beds, one may sleep restlessly, expecting to find the other bed occupied by morning. But sleeping restlessly in a Holiday Inn is far better than accepting the invitation of a campaign worker to stay at home with him. Such workers, while well intentioned and loyal, sometimes consider mattresses to be as permanent and unchangeable as the principles of the Democratic party. Almost eternal, that is to say. And even with new mattresses gratefully received, the candidate runs the risk of predawn discussions with the campaign worker about, say, the practicality of mutually assured nuclear deterrence.

A marginal risk, and one that must be accepted, is the rite of shaking hands at factory gates. It should be done while the workers are heading into the factory; the politician who stands at the gate at the end of the day will find himself, like a flaming sword, in the way of a tired worker who wants to go home, or—chancier still—between a thirsty man and his pub. The risk of plant-gate campaigning comes not from the unconvinced—people who aren't going to vote for you sidle quickly by. The danger is posed by your supporters, who will wring, squeeze, and pump your hand with slight regard to metacarpal alignment. At the end of the 1968 campaign, my doctor told me that I had a bad case of tennis elbow. Odd, I thought, since I had not picked up a racket once during the whole campaign. Then I remembered the arm-wrestling at those factory gates.

One learns on the long campaign trail that there are places where a politician may not be welcome. Beauty parlors, where tangle-haired voters shrink from your grasp, are an example. Drugstore campaigning also has its limitations. Customers there are often buying things for highly personal reasons. When sorting through corn plasters, denture adhesives, or trusses, they may not value the interruption of a politician asking, "How are your corns today?"

At the end of the trail, there is the problem faced by most political hopefuls: how to deal with defeat. After a fourth-place finish in Wisconsin in 1972, Ed Muskie said, "Winning isn't everything, but losing isn't anything." Dick Tuck, best known as a political prankster, faced his defeat in a California election by saying, "The people have spoken, the bastards." It matters most, I suppose, whether the defeat is intermediate or ultimate. Along the way, a candidate can tell his supporters, after a loss, say, in Indiana, "It's on to Michigan!" After a loss in Nebraska, one can try, "We will now hit the Oregon Trail." A loss in the East can bring forth Horace Greeley's "Go West, young [or old] man." Sallies like these will bring cheers from supporters, sometimes heartfelt, sometimes hollow. The candidate may also be tempted to drag out excuses or explanations, as if there were a difference between them: "We ran out of time." "The third candidate made the difference." "The weather was bad on election day." "The press coverage was inadequate."

Then there is the inevitable morning-after press conference with the ineluctable questions: "Are you ready to throw your support to another candidate?" "Do you look upon yourself as a spoiler from now on?" Reporters forget the answers almost immediately, but, from generation to generation, they do not forget the questions.

Vision of defeat: the abandoned campaign headquarters, with posters looking like broken kites; pamphlets and pictures strewn on the floor; crushed straw hats, plastic cups, the debris of American politics. In the room where the candidate and his top advisers waited out the results, morning dawns on the remains of the night's cocktail party, set up to celebrate the joy of victory but used to ease the pain of loss.

The most memorable morning-after for me was in the Cornhusker Hotel in Lincoln, Nebraska. I had lost the Nebraska primary of 1968, a defeat I had thought almost certain after two campaign stops. One was at a university and the other in the heart of the land of *O Pioneers!* My references to Willa Cather stirred no response.

Next to the hotel was the headquarters of a fundamentalist religious group. On the roof of their building was a red neon sign that night and day intermittently asserted JESUS BLED FOR YOU. From the building, again throughout the night and the day, hymns were not exactly broadcast but rather allowed to leak out.

The sun does not seem to rise over the prairies of Nebraska. The land sinks, and the sun is waiting. The flat light of the morning, of that particular morning, showed in the suite the remains of the previous night's indulgence. In the bowl that had held crisp crevettes on ice, only a few limp shrimp remained floating in the apologetic water. Scattered around the room, like specimens in an abandoned laboratory, were half-empty glasses of Scotch and bourbon. They stood among plates smeared with the remains of cocktail sauce.

Defeat in politics, even relative failure, is not easy to accept. Dismissing the troops, as both Napoleon and Robert E. Lee learned, is not easy. Soldiers do not want to take their horses and mules and go back to the spring plowing.

It is better to win.

A Festival of Hope

One should not take Christmas for granted, despite the fact that it has managed to survive "Jingle Bells" and even "I Saw Mommy Kissing Santa Claus."

It has survived Biblical scholarship that questions the time and place of the Nativity and raises doubts as to whether or not the Three Wise Men ever went to Bethlehem, and the new theology that says Easter's religious mystery is of greater significance than that of Christmas.

It has survived civil-liberties organizations pledged to eliminate the observance of Christmas from schools, and has so far withstood the threat of artificial trees and plastic ornaments.

Its strength lies in the fact that Christmas is a celebration of hope, and hope dies hard. Hope is a special virtue of children and a special need of adults.

Hope is very difficult to describe or to represent in sign or symbol. One can only work around it, leaving empty spaces to be filled by hope.

There are five or six important guides that, I believe, would help protect and preserve Christmas as a festival of hope.

The first is that the tree should be real. It should threaten to fade and lose its needles before the end of the holiday season. The ornaments should not be plastic or permanent, but should be fragile and breakable. One or two should be broken each year. The rest should be saved, carefully packed from year to year.

The wrapping of gifts with special Christmas paper—a practice that developed to its present strength during the Depression, when people had little to give—should be continued. It is, I think, also a good practice to save paper and boxes from one Christmas to the next, in anticipation of sending presents, even though the paper or boxes in most cases are not reused. The saving of them is an act of hope.

There are no set rules for gifts to adults; but as to children's gifts, there are some worthy of note.

Obviously, there should be toys, but among those toys should be one or two that will not last much beyond the Christmas season. A drum for a boy, as an example, which he will play knowing that it will not last long and knowing also that it may well be the last drum he will ever be given.

There should be at least one gift that cannot be used until another season, thus giving in winter a dream of spring or summer or fall.

I am against new pets as Christmas gifts. Old pets are fine at Christmas, but new pets are a distraction and, in any case, deserve separate attention.

In cold climates, at least one gift should be something to keep one warm.

Other holidays appeal to one or two of the senses, but Christmas appeals to all five: taste with its special foods; and touch with fire and warmth; and hearing with music;

and sight with trees and tinsel. More than any other holiday, it also respects the sense of smell. Among the three gifts brought to Bethlehem by the Wise Men, the Scriptures tell us, two—frankincense and myrrh—appealed to the sense of smell. So Christmas should be remembered for the scents of pine, oranges, ginger, and cloves.

One must be very careful of Christmas.

Defense of the Irish

Again this year, I resolved that I would not write about Ireland or about the Irish on Saint Patrick's Day, or certainly not go out of my way to do so. All was going smoothly, and then the remarks of one Mr. Barrington, the United States's press attaché in Dublin, were made public. Barrington did not find much in Ireland to his liking.

Only a slight flurry in the press followed his remarks. The United States Ambassador to Ireland immediately attempted to smooth things over by saying that the Irish have a great sense of humor (which they do have) and that they are very forgiving (something that I have not noted as a distinguishing mark among them). He said that he hoped the whole thing would be soon forgotten (something not likely to happen). Perhaps the Ambassador, who knows the Irish both in Ireland and in America, spoke under the protection of diplomatic immunity, which does not require at all times the whole truth.

There was no formal note of protest from the Irish government, possibly because Mr. Barrington was scheduled to be transferred from his post in Ireland, by report, to one in Japan.

As a matter of principle, or of principles, Barrington should not have been allowed to get off so easily. First, and least serious, because it was unbecoming for a diplomat to criticize the people of his host country. Second, because the Irish of all people are not in need of outside criticism. Possibly the Italians are, and the French, who seem quite pleased with themselves; and the Germans and the British, who are generally not very self-critical but often are critical of the United States. The Irish, on the contrary, have nothing but good words for America, and are of all peoples most critical of themselves. In fact, criticism of the Irish by the Irish is a growth industry in Ireland. It is a part of the gross national product and helps their balance of payments. It is encouraged by special tax exemptions granted to authors; writers—novelists, playwrights, and poets—have built careers, if not fortunes, on criticism of their own.

Third—and this is the most serious fault in the Barrington case, which might have been tolerated if it had been marked by style or subtlety—was not to match that of masters like Joyce, or O'Casey, of Austin Clarke or Patrick Kavanagh, but that of the Irishmen of the street. For example: I was in Dublin some fifteen years ago, having dinner with Sean O'Faolain, who had just published a book about Ireland. He had been, he said, stopped on the street on the way to dinner by an Irishman who inquired as to whether the book was doing well, commercially. On being assured by O'Faolain that it was, he commented, "Well, I'm glad, Sean, to know that you can still sell us."

Or the observation of the headwaiter in a restaurant just off O'Connell Street in Dublin—where I had gone with others to be warmed up after watching the military parade on the fiftieth anniversary of the 1916 Easter uprising—who asked us whether we had noted the jets flying over the parade. We answered that we had, upon which he asked, "How many did you count?" We had counted four, we said. To which he responded, "So did I. There must have been a stranger among them, because we only have three."

With observers and critics like these loose on the street, comments from the likes of Barrington are, as my grandmother would have said, "uncalled for."

Finally, Barrington is to be faulted for the substance of his criticism. Barrington is from Massachusetts. In fact, I think there is a town named after some of his ancestors. Undoubtedly affected by the Cromwellian strain that has come on down in that state through the Puritans, he did not like the "soft" weather of Ireland. He did not like the food. Who is one from Puritan New England to talk of food?—an area that has made as its principal contribution to the joys of the dinner table codfish, and the blandness of a New England dinner, neither of which can compare with Irish salmon or with Irish stew.

Barrington, in Japan, may be happier. He can have raw fish rather than poached salmon or broiled trout from the black streams that rise in the high, windy bogs. He can have rice instead of potatoes, boiled, mashed, fried, or served in potato cakes, in potato pancakes, or in that highest and most respectful treatment of the potato, "*boxty.*" He can have soybean patties rather than Irish beef and lamb, and drink sake instead of Guinness or Jameson's Irish.

Not Even a Smile

Administrations come and go. I have seen the passage of seven, from that of Harry Truman to that of Jimmy Carter. The Republic has survived each and all of them, although its condition has not been improved by all, and a few have left it in worse shape than it was in when they came to power.

For better or worse, and even when there was not much change, each administration from Truman's through that (short though it was) of Gerald Ford left some mark and memory.

Truman left the Marshall Plan, the commitment to NATO and the United Nations, and the beginning of civil rights legislation. The mark of his personality lived on. Some of his cabinet members continued as politically significant after their service in his administration ended. One or two are still in Washington.

Dwight Eisenhower left a pleasant glow, and the covenants of John Foster Dulles, which later administrations accepted as obligations, legal and moral. Eisenhower also left the legacy of the military-industrial complex, which developed during his eight years in office, but which he warned of in his farewell address, one of his best. Some of his cabinet members carried on as public personages after Eisenhower.

The Kennedy administration left its mark in style, in continuing family involvement in politics, in the consequences of the invasion of Cuba and the missile crisis, and in other ways. Members of the Kennedy cabinet continued in the Johnson cabinet, and some continue today to be active in public service, as in the case of Robert McNamara, until recently head of the World Bank, Larry O'Brien as head of the National Basketball Association, and Dean Rusk as a teacher and lecturer on international law and foreign policy. The Johnson administration made its historic mark in the escalation and pursuit of the Vietnam war, the passage of major civil rights legislation, in its contribution to the dilution of the Democratic party, and in the beautification of the city of Washington, principally through planting encouraged by Lady Bird.

The Nixon administration left the nation the heritage of Watergate, its flotsam and jetsam, the mark of the Nixon personality, and the continuing presence of Henry Kissinger, among other persons and things.

The Ford administration, although transitional and short-lived, did leave a mark. President Ford is not forgotten, although his public appearances on golf courses and on the ski slopes get about the same amount of attention as do his political appearances or statements. The Helsinki Accords, approved during his administration, are a continuing force for judgment against Russia.

The Carter administration's passing was different from the others. It might be described as the "administration that never was." Certainly, it never took on a definable and identifiable form. Neither did it make a significant mark on United States domestic or foreign policy. The administration, in retrospect, appears as a confusion of contradictions, of vacillation, of moralizing in a cloud of adverbs, with its ending lost in the return of the hostages in the middle of the inauguration of Ronald Reagan.

Many, I am sure, had hoped for a better going for Jimmy Carter. That he might at least have gone somewhat as did the Cheshire cat of *Alice in Wonderland*, leaving the remembrance of the smile, a sign of goodwill and openness.

It was not to be so. The ending came as shown in home television tapes released by the White House (one wonders why) showing the President getting ready to go to the inaugural ceremony, concerned, it appeared, about his need for a haircut, and asking that his handkerchief, his comb, his pocketknife, and cross be sent to him in the Oval Office.

Most of the members of his cabinet have disappeared. The former Secretary of State Cyrus Vance has surfaced in an article not on foreign policy, but on reforming the electoral reforms. The former Vice-President, Walter Mondale, in a recent speech, notes as one of the achievements an institutionalization of the Vice-Presidency, comparing the change with a reversal of the process by which the appendix in the human body atrophied.

Two members of the administration have announced that they intend to stay in Washington: Mr. Rafshoon, the President's public-relations man, and Mr. Caddell, his poll-taker.

What is left, at least as it is being presented, comes close to Abraham Lincoln's description of a scene after a politician he knew had left, as "floating about on the air, without heft or earthly substance, just like a lock of cat-fur."

Equality and Baseball: A Lost Cause

The drive toward equality that de Tocqueville warned us was inherent in democracy has already shown strongly in fields such as income and education. It is now threatening the last bastion of inequality, major league baseball.

The controlled inequality exercised over the game through the reserve clause, whereby players were held practically as indentured servants, was shattered by the Supreme Court decision that outlawed that arrangement, and set the stage for the free-agent bidding competitions of recent years. The old basis for inequality, which enabled the Yankees, for example, to protect and keep players practically for generations, being destroyed, a new potential for inequality in the open-market purchasing of free players was opened up.

Now, it seems that if baseball owners have their way—at least as I interpret their position as explained by Bowie Kuhn—by about the year 2000, teams in the major leagues will be so evenly matched that most games will either be settled by one-run margins or end in ties. New scoring methods may have to be introduced to determine pennant winners: a composite, say, of runs scored, a run being given four points; a runner advanced to third would be scored three; two points for getting to second base, and one for getting to first, with subtractions for players who get caught off base.

In order to achieve this equality, the current practice of giving a team that loses a first-line player in the free-agent market a top draft choice was introduced. Obviously, this method is not working, and is not likely to work in the discernible future.

The number of top baseball draft choices that turn out well as major league players is in no way comparable to the numbers that succeed in basketball or football. Prospective professional-quality basketball and football players can be detected early. Some are claimed in high school. It may not be long before they are claimed by professional teams in grade school, possibly as infants, or even before birth, as is the practice in buying prospective race horses.

There is little evidence that baseball players breed true. Although there are a few sons of major league players scattered through the big leagues today, the sons seldom, it seems, are quite as good as were their fathers.

Acknowledging that the draft will not achieve equality among the teams, the baseball owners are advocating more direct methods, something called compensation. According to this method, if a team buys a good player, a free agent, it will have to compensate the previous owner of the player by offering a player of comparable skill or usefulness, not necessarily a pitcher for a pitcher, but a player judged to be comparable by someone or by some committee. Money may be added.

Teams, according to one compensation plan, will be divided into three classes. A team buying a player from a third-class team would have to offer in exchange a better player than if the purchase were made from a second-class team. A third-class team buying a free agent out of the first-class-team category, on the contrary, would not have to offer as good a player as it would if it bought a free agent out of the second-class group, and so on.

Players also are being separated into groups and graded, beginning with those who are considered "premium" players (the opening grade for beef, followed by choice, good, canner, and cutter).

Sorting out all of these things and persons may be too much for the baseball community itself. The sorting and grading and rating may have to be assigned to independent bodies, more experienced agencies or persons—the Internal Revenue Service, say, or the Subcommittee on Separation of Powers of the Senate Judiciary Committee, which recently decided by a 3-to-2 party-line vote that life begins at conception, thus for the time being bringing to a halt, if not an end, a debate that has drawn the attention of physiologists, philosophers, and theologians for many centuries.

The compensation system, no matter how skillfully handled, will not work. It will merely put off the day of reckoning. If equality, or near equality, is to be reached in baseball, more direct and immediate actions will have to be taken. Fast base-runners, base-stealers like Maury Wills, for example, will have to be handicapped by carrying extra weight, in the manner that horses are handicapped so as to make horse races more even. Batters who have a record of not striking out often may be allowed only two strikes. Poor hitters, those that strike out often, might be given four strikes. More drastic action may be necessary, such as we took in sand-lot games when I was a boy. There was one boy who would be taken into a game only if he was given four strikes each time he came to bat, and if his outs did not count against his team.

Good hitters with high levels of runs batted in might be handicapped as are polo players, say, by having any run they bat in count as only a half-run, or by not counting the first run batted in in any game.

The last recourse in the drive for equality could be to put all the players of both teams set to play into a pool before each game. Have the managers do hand-over-hand on a bat to see which one gets first choice and then choose up sides.

The game will still be unequal.

A Real Crisis:
Double Bourbon on
the Rock

The news media evidently have become so conditioned by their habit of labeling nearly every natural or political disorder and conflict a crisis (Mount Saint Helens, Three Mile Island, Afghanistan, Presidential and papal assassination attempts, for example) that they are unable to identify a pure crisis when one occurs.

It is a welcome relief in the confusion and chaos of modern diplomacy and international controversy to have a clean, historically based crisis, such as that which has been precipitated (true crises are usually precipitated, by provocations) by the refusal of Don Juan Carlos de Bourbon y Bourbon, King of Spain, and his wife, Queen Sophia, to attend the wedding of Prince Charles of England and Lady Diana.

The Spanish King and Queen were willing to pass over and disregard ancient differences between Spain and England until the British government or the royal family announced that the second leg or lap of the royal honeymoon would begin on the royal yacht, *Britannia*, sailing from the harbor of Gibraltar.

Now, as everyone knows, with the possible exception of the British, Spain has been demanding openly for the last twenty years that Gibraltar be returned to Spain, so the historical territorial integrity of Spain may be restored.

Gibraltar, as everyone knows who watches the evening television news, was captured by the British in 1704, in the early years of the War of the Spanish Succession, and settled on England by the Treaty of Utrecht, which ended that war in 1713.

Twenty years ago, as a member of the U.S. Senate, I was asked by the Spanish Ambassador to the United States for an appointment. The topic of discussion was revision of the Treaty of Utrecht, which, he pointed out, was almost 250 years old. At the time, there was talk of revising the United Nations Charter and treaties that were twenty years old. The hoped-for revision was the return of Gibraltar to Spain. The Ambassador patiently pointed out to me that this could be done without opening up the whole of the 1713 treaty, which in some of its provisions might have cast doubt upon Don Juan Carlos's legitimacy as king, if the talked-about restoration of the monarchy went through.

The British Foreign Office must be faulted either for carelessness or for its lack of sensitivity to history, especially in dealing with Spain, where the past is more than the present, the shadow more than the reality.

Because of this bit of bad planning, a genuine crisis may develop among the remaining kings and queens of Europe. Their titles may be challenged, their legitimacy questioned. The old divisions, based principally on religion and family, may be stirred, for it was in the Treaty of Utrecht that the claims of most of European royalty were at last clearly legalized, or documented.

The Bourbon line was recognized, as was that of the Hapsburgs. The English House of Orange achieved greater credibility as the royal family of England, although that credibility was short-lived, and it was to be replaced by another German line, the Hanovers, the progenitors of the present British royal family. The Hohenzollerns were given a big lift, and the Duchy of Savoy made a kingdom, thus establishing the base from which came the later kings of Italy.

The return of Gibraltar, if it had been done quietly and unobtrusively, might have left all of these titles and continuing claims to royal status of the various families undisturbed.

Otto von Hapsburg, who was not invited to the wedding, and who has never relinquished his claims to all of the old Hapsburg empire, may rise again. The claims of the Prince to the English throne may be subject to question, since the Hanoverian line was first recognized by Act of Parliament when it chose George I as king in 1714 as the first non-English-speaking monarch of the realm. The Stuarts may reassert their claim, even though they have had no Pretender to the throne since the death of Charles Edward Stuart in 1788.

And Don Juan may find himself in trouble, for under the terms of the Treaty of Utrecht, the crown was given to his ancestor Philip V, the grandson of Louis XIV, making him the first Bourbon king of Spain on the condition that the Bourbon crowns of France and Spain should never be united.

There has not been a true monarchy in France since 1830, but royal blood runs on. There is a possibility that the genealogists might find that Don Juan has too much French Bourbon blood to meet the terms of the 1713 agreement, for he is, according to his title, both "de" Bourbon and "y" Bourbon, a blend.

There are at least two other complications, possibly mini-crises, that may arise unless this rising crisis can be quelled or quashed. The outstanding general of that war was Lord Marlborough, now of cigarette fame. Undoing the work of that war by ceding Gibraltar back to England might undermine the Marlborough advertising campaign. And of even more serious concern, the fall of Gibraltar or the surrender of it might shake confidence in Prudential Life Insurance.